OMS At A Glance

OMS International (formerly The Oriental Missionary Society) was founded in 1901 by a Chicago telegrapher, Charles Cowman, and a Japanese evangelist, Juji Nakada. They were joined in 1902 by E. A. Kilbourne. Their work in Japan was noted for its emphasis upon training of national workers, establishment of indigenous churches, and massive Scripture distribution.

For more than 87 years, OMS International has based its world evangelization efforts on three emphases: evangelism, church planting, and training Christian leaders. Today 469 missionaries (including candidates) and 3,407 national workers in 14 countries pour their energies into work contributing to these goals.

Missionaries from six nations minister with OMS in Brazil, Colombia, Ecuador, France, Greece, Haiti, Hong Kong, India, Indonesia, Japan, Korea, the Philippines, Spain, and Taiwan.

Some 3,000 students prepare for Christian ministry in our 16 OMS-related seminaries and Bible schools. These institutions provide a variety of programs from lay training to graduate degree study. Many students work in evangelism schemes known for nearly 50 years as Every Creature Crusades and patterned after the ten missionaries and their teams of Japanese workers who carried the gospel to every home in Japan in 1917. Today 140 ECC teams worldwide hold meetings and visit homes with their good news. God blesses their efforts with an average of over two new churches established each week.

OMS INTERNATIONAL, INC.
Post Office Box A
Greenwood, Indiana 46142
317/881-6751

FROM THE
CLAWS
— OF THE —
DRAGON

CARROLL F. HUNT

Foreword by Ruth Bell Graham

Special Edition
OMS International, Inc.,
P.O. Box A
Greenwood, Indiana 46142

From the Claws of the Dragon
Copyright © 1988, 1989 by Carroll Ferguson Hunt

The Francis Asbury Press is an imprint of Zondervan Publishing House, 1415 Lake Drive, S.E., Grand Rapids, Michigan 49506.

The old spellings of Chinese names are used because many of the events in this book take place in the pre-Pinyin era of Chinese culture.

Library of Congress Cataloging in Publication Data

Hunt, Carroll Ferguson.
    From the claws of the dragon : a story of deliverance from the Chinese Red Guards / Carroll Ferguson Hunt.
        p.   cm.
    ISBN 0-310-51511-4
    1. Lee, Harry, 1925–   . 2. Evangelists—United States—Biography.
3. China—History—Cultural Revolution, 1966–1969. 4. Hung wei ping.
5. China—Church history—20th century. I. Title.
BV3785.L33H86   1988
272'.9'0924—dc19   88-14704
[B]   CIP

Edited by Joan Johnson
Designed by Ann Cherryman

Printed in the United States of America

92 93 94 95 / CH / 12 11 10 9 8 7 6 5

"The Chinese dragon, worshiped and revered, has always been regarded as a benevolent creature. When angered, however, it is well to take shelter from its wrath."

Hong Kong Standard
15 February 1988

It takes ten years to make a tree, one hundred years to make a man.

Chinese proverb

Foreword

China interests us all, especially since President Nixon's historic visit in 1972. As Christians we wonder about our fellow believers and how they fared under persecution during the difficult period of the Cultural Revolution.

This story tells us of one man who seemingly wasted his most productive years in prison. But what we would call waste was really a tracing of the evidences of God's love. God didn't take Harry Lee out of his difficulties, but taught him how to endure, to survive—how to find sustenance in Scripture and hymns stored in his heart; how to pray when he was forbidden to pray; how to hold on, to bear yet another day when nothing but his stubborn trust in God stood between him and hopelessness.

You will probably read this story through in a single sitting, and your perspective on what really matters will be altered permanently.

Ruth Bell Graham
Montreat, North Carolina
10 February 1988

Chapter 1

Granny squinted as she smoothed Harry's hair one more time. The amah hovered, awaiting the old one's verdict.

Clothes? Wrinkle free and spotless.

Hands and nails? Untainted by dirt from the alley.

Handkerchief? In place.

"Call the rickshas," she flung over her shoulder as she headed toward the door. She knew the amah would scuttle out ahead of her to see that both conveyances awaited her and her grandson at the gate.

Granny stepped into the first ricksha and pulled Harry onto her black silken lap. The amah, conscious of her responsibilities as nursemaid and servant in the House of Lee, boarded the second as the pullers, leg muscles bunching, joined the whirl of Shanghai traffic.

Granny glanced at Harry, now almost six years old, her mouth and eyes softening with love. Absorbed by the street life that flowed past, the boy sat immobile and silent. Today was the pronounced day for Harry to meet a new world, a world beyond the familiar, secure home he loved.

"It is time he went to school."

So she, the Lee family matriarch, had spoken to Harry's father that morning. The matter was then settled, as such matters were always settled in honorable Chinese families.

School. Did he know what school was? Probably not, the old woman surmised. But he was bright, quick, and capable of mischief. The charms of house, garden, toys, and docile

9

servants were losing their hold on him; time had come for something more.

"*Jou-kai!* Make way!"

With a shout at the vendors of notebooks and candy, the ricksha pullers drew up before a pair of high iron gates.

Harry jumped to the ground and ran to peer between the bars. Beyond them lay a wide, empty playing field. From the left drifted the sounds of rote recitation by invisible children shut in behind the blank windows of a high gray building.

A gateman fumbled with the stubborn bar that locked the gate as Granny drew her favorite grandchild toward the opening.

"No!" the little boy screamed. He dug his heels into the gravel of the entrance and twisted in his grandmother's grip, his body bowed into an arc of protest and fear.

"What's this?" The matriarch stiffened. Two spots of red flamed in her ivory-skinned face. The vendors snickered at Harry's rebellion. Granny beckoned the amah, who clamped her hand onto the boy's wrist and yanked him toward the gate.

Bellowing, Harry twisted and jerked against their efforts to drag him into the school.

No match for his determined resistance, the two women gave up. Harry wrenched free from Granny's wrinkled grasp and clambered up into the ricksha, tears wetting his shirt.

"Go home!" he shrieked at the man standing between the shining shafts. "Go home now!"

The two pullers and the amah waited with eyes downcast, unwilling to cause Granny further loss of face by any flicker of acknowledgment of her predicament before the street's riffraff. The old woman stepped into the lead ricksha, mouth grim, eyes hooded.

The pullers turned and headed back toward the gates of the House of Lee while Harry sat rigidly on Granny's lap, sobs subsiding into sniffles.

Ignoring the street loungers who had watched them depart such a short time before, Granny stalked across the garden and into the house without meeting her daughter-in-law's questioning eyes.

Harry trailed behind her, uncomfortable with Granny's disapproval and anxious to see what she would do about it. The boy's father looked up at the sound of his mother's walking stick upon the floor.

"Ah. Today Harry began school, didn't he? How did you get along?"

Granny allowed her anger and embarrassment to blaze for an instant as she looked at her son.

"Your child," she spat, "refused to stay. He cried and ran away. He doesn't want an education. He wants to be nothing more than a day laborer!"

HARRY SHADOWED Granny after her outburst to his father, wondering what effect his behavior at the school gates would have on their relationship. That he was her favorite he knew. And he dearly loved every line in her face. After all, she had assumed responsibility for him since birth, which, he knew, had caused great joy in the Lee clan and great satisfaction for Granny.

"You've a young master in the house!"

So Harry's birth was announced. He heard the story again and again of how his grandaunt, who had delivered him, presented him swaddled in a pair of Grandfather's trousers to his father and grandparents. The use of trousers was a play on Chinese words: "trousers" and "prosperity" share the same sound, *fu*, in Cantonese, so the first Lee boy baby of his generation made his appearance in apparel honoring his masculinity and predicting his future.

But future was not in Harry's thinking when he fought

against the amah and Granny at the dreaded school entrance. Punishment loomed as the only possible explanation for such a gloomy place.

It must be a prison, the little boy thought. If not, why didn't the children run and play on the wide playing field that stretched out beyond the iron-barred gates? Why were they shut in behind those high, gray walls, droning on and on?

Freedom had characterized life for Harry. As Granny's pet he enjoyed her perpetual attention, whether it meant special food because of early allergies or a red packet of money during their Chinese New Year's celebration. Life had been good to Harry Lee.

The Lees were a typical Shanghai family. They led an insular life. They knew the many comforts that Shanghai, a foreign trade center, offered. This opportunity for wealth, however, was not as well known in other parts of China.

These other areas were erupting with change when Harry Lee was born in November 1925. The Ching dynasty, China's last, had collapsed. The Middle Kingdom had struggled to become a republic because of Sun Yat-sen's activism. Students called for a revolution. It was as if the Chinese dragon stirred from sleep.

Then there was Japan. Her manufacturing and military capabilities made her the most important power in Asia. Sensing she could make great gains from China's shifting factionalism, she constantly threatened the borders of her gigantic neighbor. To Japan, China possessed the land she needed.

Within China two men, once allies, were drawing followers into one camp or the other. Chiang Kai-shek and Mao Tse-tung disagreed on the form that China's republican dream should take. Their confrontation would change the face of China forever; its outcome would send Harry Lee into years of agony and heartbreak.

But for now the idyll still held for the Lee family. The

major issue in the home remained what to do about Harry's education. The family conferred.

"Let's try my old school, the English school," Harry's father suggested.

Granny agreed. Though inextricably rooted in Buddhism herself, she saw great value in the Christian-based teachings of the foreigners. Her son, Harry's father, embraced Christianity. Even though this meant there would be no more ancestral worship when she was gone, Granny accepted it. She liked the morals, the ethics, and the behavior of her two granddaughters, Harry's cousins; she thought her beloved Harry should learn them, too. Her treasure deserved the best Shanghai had to offer: He would attend the Public & Thomas Hanbury School.

The Public & Thomas Hanbury School was one of the municipal schools in Shanghai's International Settlement. The settlement had its own municipal council, an independent government constituted from various nations. This unique format was established because in earlier times China struggled with a xenophobic need to contain and control the foreign powers clamoring for trade and right to travel. Property concessions were made to British and French residents to lease by modest payments from their governments. Foreign law took precedence over Chinese in these treaty port concessions, and no one paid taxes to his host state.

The Shanghai International Settlement was formed by merging the British and American areas in this largest Chinese city. The resultant privileged community maintained its own utilities and education systems, enjoying a higher-than-average standard of living as they shaped China's developing commercial interests.

The House of Lee, although Chinese in custom and language at home, was part of the settlement because each of

Harry's paternal great-grandmothers had married Americans and joined the commercial life of China's treaty ports.

So when Mr. Lee suggested that Harry go to the settlement's British school, he may have spoken in Chinese but he suggested his firstborn be educated in Western thought, philosophy, and literature . . . in British English.

SCHOOL AGAIN. Harry stood quietly as Granny twitched at his clothes and brushed his hair back from his forehead.

We'll see, he thought. *I can always run away again if I don't like it.*

Cousin Margaret took his hand and smiled him toward the ricksha. The Public & Thomas Hanbury School was divided into boys' and girls' schools; since the kindergarten met in the girls' division, the responsibility of luring Harry in fell to her.

Once there, Harry lingered with Margaret for a moment, then wandered into the room where children played with blocks, tin soldiers, and a tiny farm with cows. The light, the colors, and the freedom attracted him and compelled him to stay.

From his place by the toy farm, Harry glanced back toward the door to check on Cousin Margaret. Gone! He gave a yowl of indignation at having been duped, expecting his protests to produce the same agitated response he received at home from Granny and the servants.

"Don't cry, Harry," spoke a gentle voice. Miss Alliston, the plump and rosy British teacher, bent down to comfort her newest responsibility. "Your cousin will come to take you home at lunch time."

Sure enough, at noon Margaret grinned at Harry from the doorway. He scampered across the room to her, beaming with relief. He had begun to wonder if this bright room was really another gateway to that first grim penitentiary they told him was school.

"Did you have a good time with us today, Harry?" Again Miss Alliston bent her face to Harry's. "Would you like to come back tomorrow to play with us?"

Harry stared back at the teacher for a long moment, weighing the lure of tin soldiers against commitment to this strange new school. He nodded at last.

Chapter 2

"*Hu-ei la, Ah-mah.* I am leaving now, Granny."

Harry turned in the doorway for one last farewell, then dashed through the gate and into the street. Dropping his bookbag onto the curb, he jerked off his navy blue cap with its embroidered school badge and ruffled impatient fingers through his perfectly combed hair.

"A sissy, that's what I look like. How can she expect me to go to school looking like this?" he muttered as he pushed an obliging lock of hair down onto his forehead.

"And this . . ." He perched his cap far back on his head. "The guys never wear their caps straight the way she wants me to."

Granny's ideas of what a proper young man from a good family did and did not do were always listened to and usually followed. But her beloved Harry, teetering on the brink of adolescence, occasionally chose to blend in with his peers at the price of not doing it Granny's way. He made his alterations, however, beyond the range of her surveillance.

On this gray morning both Granny and Harry's mother had tried to persuade him to wear his coat for protection against the wind that blew in off the sea.

"You will catch your death of cold," they warned, but Harry shook his head and ran off before they could insist.

Harry wanted to pit himself against whatever weather came along without huddling behind windows, doors, coats, or umbrellas. Toughness. Endurance. These qualities he reached for without knowing why. In winter he left the north window open over his bed at night and grinned with pleasure when cold rain wet his upturned face. He stood outside on the front platform of Shanghai trams when all his friends chattered together inside out of the wind. He was the first to remove his coat in the spring and the last to accept its warmth in winter.

Not only did he restyle his hair outside the gate of his home, but he also pushed his gray woolen socks down around his ankles for the run to school. *This'll toughen my calves,* he thought.

Harry had discovered athletics as he worked his way through the lower forms of Public & Thomas Hanbury School. To run, to jump, to kick away the soccer ball, to swat a home run in softball—all these were the keenest joys he had ever known. He felt that everything he did must contribute to improving his skills or strengthening his body.

With his hair, cap, and socks finally adjusted acceptably, Harry scooped up his books and continued toward school. Not tall, but well-built and agile, the boy lifted his chin and lengthened his stride, his blue school blazer settled smoothly across his young shoulders.

It was Monday, inspection day, and Harry felt ready. Dad had showed him just this morning how to adjust his necktie so it hung perfectly straight against his white shirt. With the school's badge embroidered in multicolored silk flashing on his blazer pocket, the boy knew he would pass the headmaster's checklist. His shoes were shined, his nails clean, his handkerchief folded away in a pocket. He felt secure, strong.

Clouds piling up fast at the edges of Harry Lee's sunny skies had not yet caught his attention. Soon, so very soon when the storm broke, he would find himself in need of that strength of spirit and body he had carefully cultivated.

But for now, when Harry's uncles discussed politics with Dad he neither heard nor understood the issues they found important. Harry did not care that Chiang Kai-shek's Nanking government floundered. He didn't care about Japanese expansion in Manchuria. It did not matter to him that Mao's ragged peasant band kept growing and plundering, that the Communists had established a headquarters in faraway Yenan on China's northwest frontier.

And when Mao's Communists and Chiang's Nationalist Kuomintang party agreed to ally their forces to resist Japan, Harry did not know how much power accrued to the Communists in those months. He was ignorant of the corruption and factionalism among the Nationalist rulers in Nanking.

At play in school one day, Harry heard his name called. Looking up, he saw his tall father watching him through the gates. Intensely conscious of Dad's proud eyes upon him, Harry ran to meet him.

"Hello, Dad." Harry panted his greeting in English. The Lee family spoke Cantonese at home and the Shanghai dialect throughout the city as needed, but English was the only way to communicate at the gates of the Public & Thomas Hanbury School.

Harry's dad, his eyes twinkling, reached into his pocket. "Here, Harry," he said. "Get yourself some ginger pop." He handed Harry a few coins and gestured toward the little shop that catered to schoolboys. Harry smiled his thanks and dashed away, eager for his treat.

DAD WAS TROUBLED. He acted strangely at times, but Harry perceived this only dimly, preoccupied as he was with studies and sports. The days were not so different at home, although he caught an occasional shadow on Mother's face.

The Lee family had grown by four—Dorothy, Jim, Alice, and Johnny followed Harry—and diminished by one. Sister

Dorothy, who carried the aura of an angel, succumbed to double pneumonia at age eight. Everyone who knew her mourned her death. But life went on for Dorothy's brothers and sisters; only Dad could not seem to recover.

Harry had discovered Sunday school and church, becoming an eager participant along with his two good friends and classmates, Vic and Larry. They all loved the activities of the congregation called the Endeavourers Church, led by Dr. Henry G. C. Hallock. Sent to China as a missionary by the Presbyterians, Dr. Hallock began the Endeavourers Church because he cared about the young businessmen he met in the International Settlement, aggressive men responsible for much of Shanghai's commerce. These men and their families, the American minister believed, needed such a fellowship to introduce them to Jesus Christ.

So Larry Klyhn, whose father was one of the small group of young men and women who founded the congregation with Dr. Hallock, drew Harry and Vic into the church that was to give Harry his deepest joys and yet cause some of the darkest moments of his life.

Vic Carlsen was the son of a Danish sea captain and a Soochow beauty. He and Larry (also from a Eurasian family) and Harry first found their common ground in Sunday school and church. Their circle of activities spread into school, where they competed with all comers for prizes in academics and sports. Their closeness gave them the name of "the Three Musketeers."

"Who do these guys think they are?" was a complaint heard among their schoolmates. Studious boys claimed that athletes' brains reside in their feet while the sports-minded ones believed that those who preferred to study wore thick glasses and did not know a soccer ball from a cricket bat. But the Three Musketeers refuted such childish wisdom and excelled in both worlds; the envious grumbles continued.

The Public & Thomas Hanbury School faced decline and

death, however, as did the security of the House of Lee. The Japanese attack on Shanghai in August 1937 forced Harry's school to move from the Hongkew district into rented space on Kinnear Road, a safer part of the settlement. He mourned the loss of his playing field more than he feared the shelling and other perils that disrupted their lives.

Harry's home also lay in Hongkew, full of Japanese residents; his school stood across the street from the Japanese Naval Landing Headquarters. As aerial bombing and street combat heated up, refugees poured into the settlement, an island of foreign control which they hoped would be immune from the conflict between China and Japan.

But Dad would not go. Beset by financial problems brought on by business ventures that failed, difficulties with his job, and the crushing loss of his little girl, Mr. Lee lost his emotional stability and his skill for making wise choices.

Granny, Mother, and the children fled first, but Dad would not budge. He brooded alone in the big house, ignoring the stutter and flash of gunfire that ravaged Shanghai.

Finally Lee's cousin, moving through the wounded city as a member of the Shanghai Volunteer Corps, forcibly took the miserable man from his home and reunited him with his displaced family.

In the two years that followed, irrevocable changes crushed the Lee family's elegant barriers of protection. Dad continued to brood over the loss of his job, the failure of his investments, and the death of his little angel, Dorothy. Added to his despondency came illness. None of the adults took time to explain this to Harry. The boy watched them shake their heads as they muttered together, their countenances dark with apprehension.

One day the Lee home was packed with relatives who

watched doctors bend over the broken man lying under silken comforters.

"There's a carriage waiting for me at the back door," Harry heard his father rasp. Granny's face grew taut, although she made no sound. Harry watched and held his breath as the doctor sought Dad's pulse. A long moment passed before he turned and spoke.

"He's gone."

Harry's throat tightened, and tears rushed to his eyes. He wheeled and raced toward the sanctuary of his room as his mother's cry of anguish and loss ricocheted through the House of Lee.

HARRY STOOD against the wall and stared at his father's bier. The boy could not acknowledge the enormity of his loss; the pain was excruciating. As he stared at the waxen face pillowed on satin he could think only of his father's nose. High, aquiline, it somehow honored Dad's American grandfather within the Chinese atmosphere of the death rites.

Mother wept, loudly at times, close by the casket.

"Hush, now," the women urged. "You must stop. Think of the child. Don't hurt yourself. There, there . . ."

Mother carried a sixth Lee child in her womb, and the family worried that her grief would mar its development.

The funeral was simple and soon done. Since Dad was Christian, Granny did not suggest that any Buddhist rituals be followed. She had acknowledged long since that those ancient traditions would die with her.

Chapter 3

Larry, Vic, and Harry decided to sit in front. They found seats there more easily than normal. The women whose prerogative it was to occupy the front row chose the last instead. Harry had heard their comments as he and his friends came through the door.

"Sit back here," they had urged each other. "He'll deafen us if we don't. Did you ever hear such a loud voice?"

Harry gazed at the American standing behind the lectern. Loud voice, eh? What would he say with that loud voice? Larry and Vic had wanted to attend the evangelistic meetings sponsored by the Oriental Missionary Society and so they had come to this building at 541 Yu Yuen Road.

Since a major part of Harry's world had crumbled about his feet, matters of the spirit grew more important to him. He loved his Endeavourers Church and his pastor. They had meant so much when Dad died and seemed to shelter him as he, along with everyone else in Shanghai, was learning what it meant to live under the conqueror's heel.

Eugene Erny stood to preach to the crowd assembled in the rooms of the OMS center. He and his family were on their way to India, and his series of meetings in this place were part of the transition from their homeland to their new mission assignment.

His voice sliced the air, his every word sharp-edged and clear. Harry understood why the women chose to sit in the back, but he liked the sound of Erny's voice. More, he liked what the American preacher had to say about the power of the Savior, the Lord Jesus. Jesus loves the world so much that He offers it redemption from sin; each person who accepts Him receives the privilege of spending eternity with Him. And for this life He offers strength of spirit and solace for every difficulty, no matter how great.

As Eugene Erny preached, tears coursed down his face. Harry watched. Something in his fourteen-year-old heart warmed and stirred in response.

He means this, Harry thought. *He cares. And if he cares this much . . . it must be true. I want to know God like he knows God. I want to love the Lord Jesus and belong to Him . . .*

But when Erny asked his listeners to stand and suggested that those who wanted to accept Christ as Savior should walk forward to pray, Harry did not move.

Even though he stayed in his place, the seeds of divine love lay imbedded in Harry's heart, watered by the tears of a man with a message. Those seeds would take root, grow, and flourish until the spiritual fruit they bore would shelter Harry Lee from hostile forces seeking to destroy him.

Several young people had attended the special meetings sponsored by the Oriental Missionary Society (now known as OMS International). Yearning to continue the fellowship and hungry to discover meaning in life, they wanted to meet again.

"Why don't we organize a youth fellowship? We could meet every Saturday." Their unspoken goal was, doubtless, to increase in the joy and power of the Holy Spirit within as the external world disintegrated around them.

Then on October 5, 1940, just before he turned fifteen, Harry Lee listened to another missionary. Meeting in the home of Jean and Dick Hassall of OMS, the Boosters Club—as they called themselves—invited Duncan McRoberts of the China Inland Mission to talk to them.

Again, an opportunity to invite Jesus into his life. Harry

Lee sat with his friends, head bowed and heart pounding. Then slowly, as tears prickled behind his eyes, he raised his hand to say, "Lord Jesus, I give myself to you. Forgive my sins, please, and become my Savior."

*
**

ANOTHER MISSIONARY had been watching Harry and his friends. He knew of their attendance at the Erny meetings; he also knew they hungered to learn more about God.

So Edwin Kilbourne—fondly known as "Uncle Bud"—invited the boys to come to his home each week for "round table" discussion. And there, in spite of war to the north and the Japanese occupation of Shanghai, they talked about such burning issues as movies, dancing, and what to do on dates.

Uncle Bud, even though he spent his boyhood in Japan, called China "the greatest of all mission fields" when OMS decided to begin work in the Middle Kingdom in 1924. He and his father, who with Charles E. Cowman was co-founder of the Oriental Missionary Society, sailed for Shanghai from Kobe, Japan, in the spring of 1925 and therefore were present to teach Harry Lee and his friends about Christian living.

At the Round Table the American missionary would let the boys ventilate about whatever topics the discussion had led them into and then, when it was time to add light to the heat, would flip open his Bible and point them to its wisdom as to how they should live as followers of the King.

In this setting Harry discovered spiritual strength to be even more vital to his well-being than the physical stamina he pursued with such dedication. He found himself unashamed to acknowledge his Lord. When schoolmates caught sight of Harry, Vic, and Larry, they would parody the Booster Club name by calling out, "Here they come . . . the boozers!" Harry found that his commitment to the infilling of the Holy Spirit protected him from anger against his tormentors. He could shrug off their taunts and get on with the business of growth, both physical and spiritual.

THE FORTUNES of the House of Lee had spiraled downward ever since Harry's father died. When hostilities with the Japanese intensified and the family found refuge in the International Settlement, good residences were difficult to find. Rents were exorbitant. Harry's mother, now responsible for the family, chose a humble little place, the place that was to become home for the Lees for many years.

But maintaining even a humble home required income, and that disappeared when the children's father died. Mrs. Lee sold a piece of property, and the family lived on that money for a long time.

A grandaunt offered to arrange a marriage for the widow and even urged that she give away the child she carried at the time of her husband's death. But Mrs. Lee refused, determined to keep her family together at all costs.

But at times the cost seemed beyond bearing, as when Harry rounded the corner one day with his brother Jim and discovered their mother haggling in the lane with a seedy-looking man.

"Leeches!" Harry muttered to Jim. The two boys stood at a distance as their mother swung open the rosewood wardrobe doors and gestured toward her husband's clothing still stored inside.

Too distant to hear the bargaining but aware of what was transpiring, Harry stood engulfed in waves of shame and anger. His family had consumed the funds from the property sale and now his mother had turned to selling their furniture and his father's clothes.

Beneath Harry's shame, however, lurked cold fear like a dark and frigid current under the surface of a sunlit lake. *Is Mother a spendthrift?* he wondered. *What will we do?*

Because of his father's death, fifteen-year-old Harry shouldered a growing sense of responsibility for his family — aged grandparents, bewildered mother, and four younger brothers and sisters.

Jim, too young yet strong and willing, found work in a bakery owned by the conquering Japanese. Alice, just entering her teens, went to work in a textile factory. Watching his little sister grow older too soon amid the machinery's clatter, Harry masked his aching heart with an impassive face.

He was teaching English here and there and trying to finish school as quickly as possible. The certificate from his beloved Public & Thomas Hanbury School was essential if he was going to find work that would provide enough money to support all the Lees who huddled in the shabby rooms they now called home.

Then in 1943 the final blow came to Harry's former way of life. Word seeped through the community that the Japanese intended to take over the Public & Thomas Hanbury School. And as their solemn-faced headmaster looked at his students one last time, Harry knew the man was destined for concentration camp. Questions troubled Harry's weary mind.

What will happen to him? Will I ever see him again?

The sad boy looked down at the paper he was holding that told anyone who cared to notice that Harry Lee had completed the course of study offered by the Public & Thomas Hanbury School and, further, that this certificate of completion was issued in lieu of the one that should have come from Cambridge University, England.

Harry turned and walked away. His father was gone. And gone with him were the comforts and joys of the House of

Lee. No more scarlet envelopes at New Year's. No more private rickshas or indulgent amahs. No more ginger pop or navy blue blazers. No more track and field events.

Even Larry and Vic were different. A gap widened between them. The Japanese rulers considered their families foreign rather than Chinese: they were accorded more freedom and allowed higher salaries. The other two musketeers did not fully realize that simple survival seemed to be slipping from the grasp of their friend.

Only God, revealed in the pages of Harry's Bible, offered any stability and hope. Would He be enough?

The House of Lee

Harry's mother, Mildred Lee

Harry Lee, Sr. (above),
in queue and the garb
of the Ch'ing (Manchu)
Dynasty during his late
teens, and (above
right) as an adult;
(right) Harry's sister
Dorothy, age eight, in
1934, the year she
died

Sisters Alice (left) and
Edith (below left);
Harry at age fourteen

Harry's grandfather (above), who died in 1942 at age eighty-six; "Granny," who died at age eighty in 1944; Harry's brother Jim

Harry sitting in a pull-cart
while the coolies take a break
during a five-day journey in
April 1945

Harry's brother Johnny

All photos on these pages
from Harry's albums discovered in a warehouse after
Harry's eleven-year imprisonment

Chapter 4

A smile tugged at the corners of Harry's mouth even though he did not sense his face had changed at all. He did realize, however, that when the sound of their singing drifted up Chapoo Road, suddenly tidying the sanctuary seemed a most worthwhile activity.

Harry's eyes swept the waiting church pews, checking for wayward scraps of paper as his slim hand resettled his necktie inside his shabby jacket.

Just as he turned toward the door it swung open. There, framed against the Shanghai night, stood Nadia, her golden hair catching the light, her eyes soft on the young man who watched her from halfway up the aisle.

"I love the sound of your singing," he said.

"It makes the long walk go faster for us."

Nadia. Gentle and graceful. Born to White Russian parents who had fled the Bolshevik Revolution. They settled first in China's western province of Sinkiang on the border of eastern Russia; later, when the Communists took over western China, they moved east and south to the outskirts of Shanghai.

Several from their community had begun attending the Endeavourers Church. They wanted fellowship with other Christians and they needed to learn English. Since services for this congregation were conducted in English, it seemed a good and profitable place to be.

Harry and Nadia met at church. Their friendship ripened

into love at the Bible studies and meetings of the youth fellowship. Sundays took on a special luster for Harry because he knew that when he went early to church to prepare for evening worship, Nadia would come. Those few sweet moments of conversation in the empty sanctuary were like a banquet spread for him alone.

A decade had passed since Harry Lee walked away from the Public & Thomas Hanbury School for the last time. During the intervening years he spent twenty months with the Nationalist guerrillas and then with the Nationalist army as a secretary, interpreter, and English-teaching officer for one of Chiang Kai-shek's generals. In those days the generalissimo's forces entertained hope that the Americans would join their struggle to drive the Japanese invaders from the country; then people with English skills would forge a vital link with such important, useful allies.

The atomic bomb dropped on Hiroshima brought the war to an end, and Harry's military service wound up in a race with Communist troops to accept Japanese surrender in town after town. As he traveled and witnessed firsthand how things were handled, Harry became disillusioned and disgusted with the corruption and mismanagement among military leaders.

Sick in body and soul, Harry persuaded his general to release him. He returned to Shanghai, but once home it seemed he had nothing to do but stand in the train station and watch his friends leave China.

Business people with connections or citizenship in the West recognized that China was no longer a safe place for them. Vic went to Denmark and Larry to England, leaving their fellow musketeer behind with a few athletic trophies, some snapshots, and a heavy heart that tried hard not to ask God why.

Why did they go? Because within a few short years after World War II ended, Japanese occupation of China was exchanged for a weak Nationalist government, only to be replaced by Communist rule. At Peking in October 1949, Mao Tse-tung proclaimed that the Middle Kingdom was now a Communist state. The clouds that once hovered at the edges of Harry Lee's world now threatened to block out the sun.*

HARRY SPENT his working hours tethered to a desk in the accounting department of what used to be the British and American Tobacco Company, Ltd. As Mao solidified his hold on China, that erstwhile foreign, capitalist firm was taken over and became the state-owned First Rolled Tobacco Factory.

But whatever its name, Harry, torn by conflict between his Christian commitment and the product he indirectly helped to market, trudged each day toward his responsibilities within the factory walls.

It isn't right, he often thought. Still the athlete, Harry believed that the Lord expected His children to care for their bodies as well as their souls. But then he, as the eldest son of his widowed mother, bore a deep sense of obligation to care for his family, his younger brothers and sisters who required food, clothing, shelter, and education. Thanks to his earnings, not only were they surviving, but Edith and Johnny, the two youngest Lees, were attending college.

Regardless of those positive results, Harry felt trapped in

---

*There were as many as 8,500 Protestant missionaries in China in the mid-twenties before civil strife and World War II drove out most of them amid increasing persecution. A brief resurgence after the war brought up to 3,000 missionaries back to the country, but all were gone by the end of 1951 due to the Communist takeover (*The New International Dictionary of the Christian Church,* ed. J. D. Douglas, rev. ed. [Grand Rapids: Zondervan, 1978], 218).

an occupation that often brought a rueful smile to his face. He and his fellow musketeers had learned accounting from Larry's father, who had insisted they needed a practical skill to balance the literature, history, and art. Good manners alone had kept Harry plugging away at the concepts Mr. Klyhn pounded into the boys' heads. Now here he sat, keeping track of debits and credits so his family might live.

As he gave his family the gift of his time and energies, Harry fed on his Lord. Any church activity found him there. Harry taught Sunday school and was ordained a deacon at age twenty-eight, a remarkable honor in a culture that usually required the young to wait for decades before being assigned places of leadership. The youth group, sensing that their nation convulsed with changes that could only harm and hinder Christians, worked at preparing themselves for the coming storm.

"Don't depend on us," a missionary had said back when the Japanese were advancing. "We won't always be here. When the Japanese come through the city gates, we shall be interned. So I suggest you divide your group into four. Take turns praying, leading singing, giving messages." The motto of the group became "Meetings by Young People for Young People."

Pressures mounted. The Communist government organized the Three Self Movement (self-governing, self-propagating, self-supporting) and issued a list of dos and don'ts regarding religious practices that the Endeavourers Church rejected, stirring up surveillance by government agents.

At work, Harry faced mounting troubles. He had to apply for permission to leave the office early to attend and conduct the weekly meetings of his church. He continued to meet with his fellow believers, a sign of open rebellion that cost him salary bonuses and earned the attention of officials bent on eradicating faith in God. But Harry's faith in his

Redeemer would not let him yield to the demands of the atheistic government.

Then in 1956, the year of Mao's disastrous Hundred Flowers campaign, a new crisis invaded the life of Harry Lee.

Harry and some fellow believers were meeting secretly in early May to celebrate the centennial of the arrival of missionary Hudson Taylor in China aboard the S.S. *Lammermuir*. At that quiet little meeting the Lord spoke to Harry, saying, "I want you to serve me full-time."

Aware that Christian ministers disappeared daily into prison to suffer torture and face death, Harry struggled with God's call.

"I have a good job with a bright future," he argued. "Must I give that up? What will become of Mother? Of Edith? Johnny? All of them? They depend on me. There's no future in the ministry now, Lord. You know that."

But Harry's love for his Lord won out. "I know you love me, Lord, and I love you. You loved me first. If you want me for this work, I am your man. You open up the way."

A verse in Hebrews summarized his commitment made that May night: "Looking unto Jesus the author and finisher of our faith; who for the joy that was set before him endured the cross, despising the shame, and is set down at the right hand of the throne of God" (12:2).

Friends, at home in China and across the seas, heard of Harry's decision. They heard and prayed. Among them was his former Sunday school teacher, Miss Elizabeth Ward, who now lived in Hong Kong.

"Harry," she wrote, "what do you think about coming to seminary in Hong Kong?"

He pondered her question. After a year, a time allotted so he felt sure he was not carried away by emotion, he applied to that seminary and was accepted. The next thing was to resign from the firm where he had worked for ten years. One does not resign easily from a state-owned company in

China; Harry's request shocked officials and aggravated the suspicion already raised against their young accountant. Employees were expected to take orders, not initiate change.

But Harry finally extricated himself from his job and walked away from the tobacco company, doubtless leaving a file bulging with reports on his unusual behavior. But God had said, "I want you, son." And Harry refused to disobey the Master, no matter what it cost.

Beginning his new career, he gave himself to two activities. One was working through the labyrinthine procedures of applying for permission to study abroad; the other, giving full-time leadership to his church.

The little group that met on Chapoo Road was decimated, however. China's Marxist government sought to impose controls on every Christian church and fellowship in the country. The Three Self Movement was its method of turning believers away from their dependence on God and forcing them to join the rest of the nation in trumpeting their self-sufficiency, thanks to Mao and no one else.

But the Endeavourers Church refused time and time again to join the movement, incurring official wrath. Surveillance, questioning, and criticism caused many to turn away, unwilling to risk their families or their freedom by being known as followers of God rather than the government.

UNMARRED JUST YET by the fear and uncertainty that tainted their world, the love between the Eurasian man and his Russian refugee sweetheart flared up brighter and stronger, perhaps more so in contrast to the gloom that surrounded them. Along with their commitment to life controlled by Jesus Christ and His teaching, the business of finding a way to leave China bound them together.

Nadia and her family were trying to go to Australia, to Canada, to some place safe where they could begin a new life out from under the burden of communism. The freedom they had sought in China as refugees from the Communist takeover in Russia had evaporated under orders from their new Marxist officials. Once again they needed to seek a haven.

Harry was still making the rounds of officialdom, papers in hand, requesting permission to study abroad. He told Nadia one evening after church of a disappointing encounter.

"After he looked over my papers, one official began questioning me about activities here at church. He wanted to know amounts of our offerings, everything. I refused to answer, telling him it had nothing to do with my application. His face closed up as if someone had pulled a curtain across a window. I don't think he'll help me."

Nadia and Harry rode the bus out toward her home Sunday nights after church. They always disembarked a couple of stops early so they could walk through the friendly darkness and talk, savoring the quiet moments alone.

Happy hours with Nadia. Meetings, Bible study, times of prayer and fellowship with the dwindling group at church. Moments of joy seasoned Harry's days as he continued his efforts to obtain permission to go to seminary.

One of the happiest of such moments came during a home visit from Johnny, Harry's younger brother, who was studying architecture in a college north of Shanghai. Harry prayed for and worried about tall, athletic Johnny, who had joined the Communist Youth League without realizing the implications of that step.

During his summer at home Harry noticed that Johnny seemed concerned about matters of the spirit. When Harry spoke to him about it, Johnny was ready. They knelt beside Harry's bed and he told Johnny how to become a Christian, free from sin's guilt. Harry taught him how to pray.

Neither brother knew how much Johnny's choice, made at that bedside, would cost him. They did know that Mao's cadres across the nation were cracking down on the freedom of speech and thought that had blossomed during the Hundred Flowers campaign. Few escaped their fury.

Neither would they.

Chapter 5

A man wearing a white coat and white surgical mask led Harry Lee to a shack out in the dreary fields of the prison farm. The door screeched on its hinges as they entered.

Inside Harry could see two bodies, one on the ground and one on a table. He drew back the shroud from the body on the table; a stab of pain pierced him. Tears poured uncontrollably, endlessly down his cheeks. But as he stared at the still, cold face he was astonished that he bore no hate, no bitterness.

Johnny was dead. The telegram had told them and here he lay, his life snapped like a piece of thread.

Harry looked at his brother's hands. They had ballooned to twice their normal size from heavy labor. Now he knew why his last letters looked as if they were written by an old man. Someone had managed to pull socks over Johnny's swollen, frostbitten feet, but his shoes, far too small, just hung from the end of his toes.

Harry had wired Jim, his remaining brother, to meet him at the Tientsin prison farm so they could take care of Johnny together. He waited three miserable days for Jim to come from his railroad job at Chuchow, wondering all the while how his beloved young brother survived that bitter place for three years.

After praying to receive Jesus Christ as Savior, Johnny had returned to his architectural studies. He soon became deeply involved in the political movement of 1957, standing up for what he believed to be right by defending teachers and students who fell under attack.

As a result, Johnny was expelled first from the Communist Youth League and finally from the university. Together with other students and those considered subversive to the best interests of the state, authorities hauled him to a prison farm. Within three years the combination of starvation and forced labor had killed him.

On the night Jim arrived at the prison farm, officials gave Harry and him a mule cart. "This used to be dangerous country, you know," the muleteer muttered as they bumped through the darkness. "Bandits everywhere. You couldn't have traveled toward town without getting your throat cut."

Harry shut out the man's grisly talk. Time and again he turned to look at Johnny's body behind him in the cart. Because this was the last ride the three Lee brothers would ever take together, he tried to etch scenes of that night into his mind for the years to come, not yet knowing that such memories stay whether one wants them to or not.

And 1959 brought yet another heartbreak for Harry Lee. Nadia and her family were granted permission to leave China; his was still denied. He faced his sweetheart one more time in the silent, empty church sanctuary, watching her tears, wanting to make it as easy for her as possible.

"Forget me," he said, although they had spoken of marriage. "I may never get out. Think about your parents."

"I want to wait for you," she whispered.

Harry struggled to harden his breaking heart so he could help Nadia be strong. He quoted a verse from Romans to her: "And we know that all things work together for good to them that love God, to them who are called according to his purpose" (8:28).

"I will pray for you," Harry promised. "I believe God can join us together someday; but if He has other plans, we must submit to His will."

Although Nadia vanished from his sight, Harry fanned one last ember of hope. They had promised to wait for each other, and Harry purposed to pray for his Nadia each day of his life until God reunited them.

Small hopes and even prayers, however, could not make the Shanghai streets less gray nor Sunday nights less bleak for him.

FROM 1959 TO 1961, China writhed under agonies she fought hard to conceal from the outside world. Starvation decimated thousands of communities. People ate tree bark and rats—and died. Mao's 1958 Great Leap Forward, touted as solving all shortages and problems by a single burst of massive energy, created instead such turmoil and misery that the Middle Kingdom seemed mortally wounded.

At the same time the Endeavourers Church entered its death throes. Because of its international character, Harry Lee's church was probably the last place in China where Jesus Christ was worshiped openly. Dr. Hallock's dream as founding pastor was to minister to influential Eurasians of Shanghai, and so the church was registered with the Communists as a foreign enterprise. This registration had bought extra time, but now that time was running out.

Government officials had regularly urged church leaders to submit to the Three Self Movement. Then church authorities had been required to hand over the deed to their property to the Communists. For this precious document they received a receipt that in later months was also taken from them. No evidence of their ownership remained.

Then came notification that "rent" on church property would go up. The government was requiring payment for the use of their facilities now that officials held deed to the Endeavourers Church. Although Harry had resigned from his church offices, which had increased as the attendance dwindled (pastor, secretary-treasurer, deacon), daily he expected notification of the amount they must pay. Impatient, he asked for information, again caring less about personal protection than pursuing what be believed to be right.

It took six months for the billing to come, and when Harry read it, he knew another dream had died. The sum demanded by the government was exorbitant; bankruptcy would end the public ministry of his cherished church.

Harry and the few remaining members of the Endeavourers Church cashed in all resources available to them to help meet the payment. They sold the heavy furniture, but kept folding chairs, a lectern, Bibles, hymnbooks—anything portable—and stowed them in friends' homes in hope that the church could reopen.

In the spring of 1961, friends and the remnant membership gathered for the final service. Because Harry's one remaining fellow deacon was his dear friend the French charge d'affaires, diplomats from the Swiss, Norwegian, and British consulates rolled up in their limousines to attend, thereby expressing their regrets over the closing of the Endeavourers Church.

Harry Lee rose to preach one last sermon before his Communist rulers took over the church. His text? From the New Testament, 2 Corinthians 5:1: "For we know that if our earthly house of this tabernacle were dissolved, we have a building of God, an house not made with hands, eternal in the heavens."

A FEW DAYS LATER Harry swung open the church doors for the last time. He watched, impassive, as several government officials entered and filed along one side of the table that had been prepared. As Harry approached the opposite side of the table, his fellow deacon from the French consulate pulled out the chair beside him. Two other church members and the caretaker sat facing the Communists who had come to take the church.

Had God brought Harry Lee to a dead end? Was this the reward for his faith, his commitment to service, his love of goodness and right?

Now that his church was gone, where could he go for spiritual sustenance? Where would he get the strength to accept the poverty that now ground down the once proud House of Lee, or the refusal of his preparation for ministry? Why was even the privilege of lay leadership in the service of his King denied him?

Dead end or no, Harry felt his spirit rise as the moment came when the Christians had to render the church keys to the Communists and relinquish their property. The spirit that refused to quit, honed on the English school's playing fields, blended in Harry Lee with the oriental ability to express one's deepest feelings by the most delicate of gestures.

As the official looked across the table toward Harry and waited, Harry looked at his adversary for a long moment, then turned and with a nod instructed the church caretaker to give the man the keys.

The official concealed his awareness of Harry's unwillingness to acknowledge defeat, glanced toward his own errand runner, lowest man in the Communist entourage, and with a similar nod instructed him to receive the keys.

Men on both sides of the table understood the refusal to give in that Harry had communicated through the exchange of the keys. And though the sanctuary now closed against him and his fellow Christians, though his efforts to leave China failed, and though Nadia's letters aggravated rather than eased the distance between them, Harry's heart, mind soul, and spirit stayed fixed on his Lord. The words spoken by Job, the biblical sufferer, became a litany for him: "Though He slay me, yet will I trust Him."

Such trust was his only shelter, because within five years a holocaust greater than anything Harry had known would rack China, setting in motion a series of events that, like a string of firecrackers, would explode in lightning succession, tossing him into a caldron destined to annihilate millions.

Chapter 6

What is a cultural revolution? The term sounds like an outburst of creativity, an onslaught of new concepts in painting and music, a renaissance of the arts. But China's Cultural Revolution, unleashed by the aging Chairman Mao, was described by one Western newsman as a "wild rampage of hate and irrationality, in which millions had been unjustly imprisoned and murdered." A revolution, yes, but one that clawed through China as if bent on destroying the rich mix of her culture.

At first Harry just watched as the Red Guards, children gone mad, dashed up and down Shanghai streets in wild parades, tearing down street signs or battering buildings that reminded them of foreigners. He saw doctors, musicians, and landowners suffer humiliation, beatings, and sometimes death.

But he knew that his spectator status could collapse at any moment. An afternoon that he, his sister Edith, and their little niece spent in the park told him this.

It all began simply enough. A visit to a friend; some hours together amid the trees and green grass, soaking up contentment and companionship. But when it came time to go home, Harry and Edith could not board the tram because of the crowds. Masses of people swirled through the streets muttering and shouting, looking for victims; a collection of individuals ready to coalesce into a mob.

Harry turned from the overcrowded tram and signaled a

pedicab. The threesome climbed in and directed the driver to take them home. They rolled through the city until the crowd thickened and blocked the street. Apprehension prickled along Harry's spine.

Just ten minutes more, Harry kept thinking as he looked at people milling around all sides of their pedicab. *Ten minutes more and we'll be home and safe.*

Just as the driver rounded a corner, someone stepped toward them pointing and shrieking. "Look here! Look at them!"

Harry sensed what was coming. Part of the Red Guard rampage focused on decadence in dress. An armband wearer could stop a man on the street, whip out a piece of knotted string, and measure the width of his trouser legs. If the pants legs proved to be narrower than the string ("hooligan trousers," they called them), the wearer could be subjected to ridicule and any kind of violence the mob decided was necessary to punish him for his bourgeois dress.

People surged around the pedicab; the child, frightened, began to cry. Harry knew that a girl in the crowd had caught sight of Edith's white shoes, and since their toes were fashionably pointed, she wanted to set the mob on this elitist trio.

Harry shoved the white shoes down out of sight, leaving Edith barefoot, and jumped to his feet. He jerked off one of his own sandals and waved it over his head.

"What's wrong with this sandal?" he shouted. "You can find them in any shop."

People turned to one another, confused by Harry's plea. "What's he saying? ... Sandals? ... I've got sandals, what's wrong with that?"

But the girls close to the pedicab turned and waved their arms at the rest of the crowd. "No!" they screamed. "It's her ..." And they pointed at Edith.

Confusion prevailed just long enough. People argued with

each other. Those at the back of the crowd drifted away at last to look for a more promising victim, and the girls who hungered for retaliation against Edith's white shoes lost the sympathy of the mob.

The crush eased and the pedicab inched through. As Edith wiped away their little niece's tears, Harry evaluated what they had just experienced: "We're going to have to be more careful if this is the way things are going to be. Our dress, our speech, even the way we walk." They were prime targets for Red Guard fury, with just enough individuality to arouse attention.

Meanwhile, neighbors were committing suicide because their homes were ransacked and their families tortured or dragged off to prison. To them, death seemed better than life like this.

THE FIRE burns closer, Harry thought as he stood at the window of their upstairs apartment and watched a neighbor's treasures blazing in the street below. Red Guards pulled out the man next door, clapped a tall, pointed dunce cap onto his head, and wrote his crimes on a placard to hang about his neck. "Capitalist, exploiter of the people," they called him. Beating a dustpan, he was paraded through the streets, his progress slowed by the beatings, kicks, and spitting of people who watched.

How safe am I? Harry wondered. *Is the Lord going to allow all this to happen to me? I haven't broken any laws, so I'm not worried about that, and yet . . ."*

Harry knew that logic and honesty had little to do with the Cultural Revolution. He also knew that his dossier contained carefully collected information that in the eyes of China's tormentors spelled guilt requiring punishment. A touch of the West in his ancestry, son of a wealthy businessman (no matter that their wealth was all gone), a

Christian who had quit his job to serve the church, and—worse—one who wanted to leave China to study for the Christian ministry.

So when Harry turned into the lane after paying a bill at the bank, he was not surprised to find a stranger lurking there. The man tossed a glance at him and turned away. *It's coming . . . oh, Lord, it's coming . . .*" kept turning in his mind.

Awareness of what lay ahead blocked out every other sensation as he climbed the stairs.

After dinner that same day, Harry heard footsteps pound up to their door. A visitor from downstairs begged to hide in the Lee apartment.

"When I went to leave," he panted, "I first looked through the slit in the gate . . . the street was full of men with red armbands, so I ran to the back . . . but there I saw another crowd just like the one in front . . . I think they want me . . . you've got to let me hide!"

Harry paused for a long moment, then he spoke. "There's no place here for you to hide . . . and besides, I think they want me. I suggest you go down, open the front gate as normally as you can, and walk out. Don't look furtive or scared—and let's hope my judgment is correct."

The man scanned Harry's face for an instant, nodded, and walked slowly back down the stairs. Harry moved again to his window and watched as the man opened the gate and moved through it.

I guess he's the happiest guy in the world right now, Harry mused. *I'm glad for him . . . but this confirms things for me.*

A parade of Red Guard atrocities marched across his memory as he listened for steps on the stairway. People driven mad, mass killings, street battles, eyes gouged out. What should he do? Try to escape? Being strong and fit, he knew he could run up to the sun-stage on the roof of their building, climb the wall, take a flight of steps on the other side, and escape.

But where could I go then? he wondered. *What would happen to our church? Or to Mother and Sister?*

Harry took a deep breath and decided. *I cannot leave. I'll stay and face them. I'll see it through, whatever happens.*

With that, Harry turned his back on the window. His niece was visiting that day with her mother, Alice. Harry drew the young girl onto his lap and began to tell her a story even as the Red Guards stormed up the stairs.

Some twenty or twenty-five young people exploded into the room and seized each family member. Then they ransacked the apartment, searching, they said, for weapons or secret radios or counterrevolutionary literature.

An early matter of business was to identify each person in the apartment. When the Red Guards discovered that Alice worked in a factory, they released her and her child. "Oh, you are a worker? You can go."

Fear and his sense of responsibility boiled up together in Harry when he heard Edith screaming from the other room. "You leave my sister alone!" he insisted. "I am the one you can question. I am her elder brother and head of this house."

Content that he had drawn the focus of their fury to himself and away from his mother and younger sister, Harry agreed to cooperate with his captors.

The search continued. They tore open ceilings and broke through walls and floors. Where were the weapons, the secret messages, the radio transmitters? They knew these Christians were up to something; all they required was evidence.

"Weapons? This is the only 'weapon' I have." Harry produced an old machete that Vic had given him.

During their search the intruders forced Harry to sit under guard in the tiny bathroom. One of the girls watched to be sure he did not escape or kill himself. But as the hours spun out, her eyes drooped and Harry could see that she was really only a child. Although he could have easily overpowered her or reported her for failure of duty, he stayed quiet. He sensed in her tinges of sympathy for his plight.

God promised never to leave His children comfortless. This Harry knew, and so the almost imperceptible kindness that breathed out from the weary girl reminded him of his Savior's steadfast love in the ordeal at hand.

The Red Guards stayed in the Lee apartment for three days and nights. After the search, questioning began. Harry had already written his "confession," admitting his church activities and responsibilities, but this was not concrete enough for their purposes.

Assigning Harry a mat on the floor as his place to sleep, they then refused to let him rest. Several surrounded him like a cartwheel surrounds its hub. Questions. Questions. Questions asked in strident voices assuming guilt, refusing plausible answers.

As soon as one set of questioners wore themselves out, they went away for a few hours' rest while a new group took their places around their victim. Asking, relentlessly accusing until the next shift replaced them.

Well, I have one advantage, Harry reflected as he responded automatically to their repetitious shouts. *The fruit of the Spirit . . . patience is one . . . I've learned patience at the feet of the Lord. These people can't understand patience. They're like tigers . . . they've got to be off . . . they can't wait. Even if they try to beat out of me what they want to hear, they will go eventually . . . I can wait.*

Sensing, finally, that they had wrung this situation dry, Harry's tormentors prepared to leave. They dumped his letters, papers, books, Bibles, and a few small valuables into two large sacks. But there remained the necessity of impressing on the neighborhood that they had performed a valuable service by tormenting Harry Lee, his aged mother, and his young sister.

One enterprising young marauder discovered in the

apartment downstairs a magazine cover portrait of Generalissimo Chiang Kai-shek, their Nationalist enemy now ensconced in Taiwan. Dragging Harry down the stairs, they perched him on a stool in the lane, this time avoiding the main street and its crowds. They shrieked to the curious few that even though "everybody is destroying pictures like these, he still keeps it. He reveres it because Chiang is his hero and the guy he worked for."

"That's a lie! It isn't mine!" Harry wanted to shout, but he patiently held his peace.

Next the Guards produced the gift machete, now polished and glinting in the light. The bystanders responded to its alleged menace as they knew they must: "First the picture, now this! He ought to be hung right away!"

Mao's little soldiers also splattered huge characters onto poster paper and plastered onto the gate their accusations against his secretaryship for the Nationalists, his reactionary religious activities, and his fraternization with foreign consulates. But as he watched them, Harry noticed that only a few dabs of glue held the poster in place, certainly not the normal amount.

Is one of them sorry? he wondered. *Are they ashamed? Do they know deep inside they have no case against me?*

The Red Guards stormed off in search of other victims at last. Harry was assigned to clean the lane, its gutters and drains and paving, as public punishment for his misdoings.

And when rain washed the accusing poster off the gate, he smiled and patted it back in place. God's grace and love held him close, giving him strength and a sense of perspective in a world gone mad.

He held on to his dream. Some day, God willing, he would train for the ministry and then be able to lead men and women to his beloved Savior.

Chapter 7

"But I don't know these people, Edith. Are you sure they can be trusted?" Harry searched his sister's pleading eyes.

"They're my friends, Harry. They know the boatmen and can arrange for us to go on the next sailing. We'd be in Hong Kong in just a few hours! All we have to do is go. Do you want to just sit here until the Red Guards come back? Let's go . . . *please?*"

The escape plan offered by Edith's friends was such a departure from Harry's normal behavior patterns that he struggled against his initial desire to reject it outright. To leave China would be a dream come true; to go buried under a load of fish in a creaking old junk entailed risks different from stubbornly working through government channels.

But hadn't he been begging God for direction about what to do next? What if his caution kept him from recognizing the Lord's plan? Maybe their scheme was the answer. The door to freedom, to seminary, to service in the name of Christ.

And then this. Harry's heartbeat quickened every time he looked at the calendar picture sent him from Hong Kong. It was a small painting of a fishing junk silhouetted against the sea. Underneath were printed words that would not leave him alone: "Launch out into the deep" (Luke 5:4).

Harry was tired of paddling in the shallows; he wanted to know more of God and more of life. If he did not act soon, the years would wear away, dotted here and there with

English students, with financial aid from friends and relatives overseas, with the constant care of his fatherless family.

The seminary in Hong Kong had been waiting for him for ten years. Surely this was divine direction to go, to take to the sea. On the stern of the junk the artist had painted the rudder in the form of the cross. "He rules the waves," it said to Harry. "He'll be in the boat with us."

CANTON. The ten fugitives tried to blend into the crowd—not easy for a ballet teacher, a plastic surgeon, a film maker's wife, a part-time actor, and several others already targeted by Red Guards for their bourgeois ways.

Harry had hidden his Western-style jacket beneath the lumpy blue Mao coat and pants of the proletariat. A white surgical mask helped to make him look like every other peasant who was trying to avoid flu germs and keep warm.

Canton. Less than an inch from Hong Kong on the map. Situated at the head of a massive bay into which pour several of south China's great rivers. Out on the coast where bay becomes sea lies Hong Kong, a tiny concession to British demands in another era; now a sparkling colony of capitalistic freedom pinned to the somber bosom of Communist China.

Cantonese was no problem for Harry. His mother came from the south, so it was her native tongue. Having spent time there with his parents years ago, he knew the language.

There were, however, problems not so easily solved. Quarrels broke out among the others as to who would go on the boat when the time came. Money issues were never resolved. They told Harry the boatmen needed more. The boatmen said the best boats were not available. Delays tightened their already taut nerves, and at times they were sure police peered at them with suspicion.

Harry felt growing apprehension. His fellow fugitives made him uncomfortable. Although the ballet teacher had spoken fondly of her Christian grandmother, she asked a fortune-teller to predict the success of their venture. This alarmed Harry, and he spoke out against this sin.

Suspicion deepened as the others asked him to raise more money, suggesting that Edith must stay behind if he did not cooperate. Torn by his desire to help people, Harry considered selling his watch, since he could borrow no more money from his Shanghai friends. Leaving Edith behind was not an option.

Canton seemed sinister. Eyes watched. Menace lurked in every public place. As he and his companions were returning to their rooms one night, Harry saw militia lined up in the road and staring at him and his companions. As he walked by, Harry could feel their eyes boring into his back.

It's as if they want us to know they suspect us, he thought. He felt as if something evil was closing in on them and he could do nothing to stop it.

Harry clung to faith in his Lord, however, even as he struggled to clear each hurdle. His heart stood fixed. Regardless of the adversary he faced in man or circumstance, his bedrock commitment to follow the Master remained unchanged.

Hope of freedom crumbled within a few days. As Harry and several of the others passed the police station at the head of the lane where they were staying, an officer called out.

"Come in here!" the officer beckoned to the ballet teacher and the person walking beside her. "We want to ask you something."

"Go quickly!" she whispered to her friend. "Tell the others to go back to Shanghai!"

The police detained one of the pair and freed the other after a time—a tactic that enabled them to discover the whereabouts of all the group, since the one they released dashed from place to place warning the others that their plan had collapsed.

Harry was arrested while visiting his Canton relatives. Officials burst into the room and ordered him to stand and be searched.

"What is going on?" his hostess demanded. "How can you be so rude to our guest?"

"Hush! Leave them alone," her husband said. Harry had told him the night before why he and Edith were in Canton and how the police had discovered their plan. "I'm taking Edith back to Shanghai tomorrow," he had said.

But instead of boarding the Shanghai train, Harry found himself walking toward the police vehicle with hands cuffed behind his back. His desire to launch out had plunged him into deeper waters than he imagined possible.

These waters would deepen more.

THE TRAIN pulled into Shanghai at night. Guarded by two plainclothesmen who had accompanied him from Canton, Harry was led through the police station and into the waiting van for the ride to the detention center.

Women police officers took Edith in another direction; the brother and sister had only a moment to say good-bye. Harry had insisted to his captors that he alone, as Edith's older brother, was responsible for their escape attempt. "Just leave her alone," he begged. "I brought her here. The blame is mine!"

But the police refused to acknowledge his pleas or to reveal what they had in mind for Edith.

At the detention center Harry was meticulously searched. Officials bent his collar between their fingers, listening for the papery crackle of hidden notes. They took his glasses, shoelaces, belt, even the drawstring from his underwear, then pushed him into a large cell and clanged the door shut behind him.

Harry peered through the gloom trying to make out what sort of place he had come to. The fourteen-foot space was half filled by a raised wooden platform built over the concrete floor for the prisoners to sit or lie on. Underneath they customarily stowed their possessions.

As Harry stumbled in and ran his hand along the platform, he felt a row of round, smooth balls. Heads! Human heads!

"Get in! Get in!" the guard shouted at him.

How can I get in without kicking this row of heads? Harry puzzled. He was troubled, too, by his unwashed condition after three days on the train plus two weeks of detention in Canton. Bathing had not been on the agenda since his capture. But yielding to pressure from the guard, he began to wiggle himself between the sleeping bodies attached to the round, smooth heads.

"Get underneath," a new voice growled.

Then Harry realized that his feet had not been kicking bundles of prisoners' possessions under the platform, but more heads. Hampered without his glasses, he fingered yet another row of what reminded him of billiard balls.

Good gracious! he mused. *In that little place . . . with all those on top . . . how many people are jammed in here?*

"You go down there!" ordered the voice from the dark.

As Harry fumbled among the lower layer of sleeping men, he found one at the end who opened his bedroll and motioned him in. Slowly he crawled into the offered space, ashamed to intrude into the man's clean blankets.

Only later did Harry learn he was being initiated onto the bottom rung of the prisoners' organizational ladder. The most recent arrival in the cell slept at the end of the lower row with the man who came just before him. After all, there had been no time for his family to bring him bedding, so the next lowest person must share with him.

Then when a man was freed or sentenced and moved from his detention center, the senior man moved up from the bottom and gained a spot on the platform while the others moved along accordingly.

Harry shared his fellow prisoner's bedroll in their new-comer's place until a greener, newer man was shoved into their common cell. By this time Harry's mother, although she did not know where he was or why, had been ordered to supply for him bedding and other items required for prison life.

The new man was a street urchin, and Harry smiled wryly as he remembered his own concern at being dirty when he arrived. *Boy, if I thought I was dirty,* he thought, *I don't know what adjective would suit this guy!*

Next morning—prisoners always seemed to come and go at night—when the men squatted together on the wooden platform, they motioned the newcomer away. His hair was long and matted, gummy with the garbage in which he dug for usable items. The powerful odor he bore cut through the packed cell like a knife blade.

"You go to the corner. Get over there. You smell awful!"

"Look," Harry interrupted. "He's got to be with us. We can't shove him away and make him sit by the toilet"—a barrel-sized wooden receptacle—"if the guards pass, they'll see we're not democratic, so that's no solution. Let's wash him, clean him up."

At Harry's instigation one man offered a bit of soap, another pulled out a towel. Several contributed part of their water ration. All participated in the renovation of the street boy; they even made him wash all his clothes.

Before his clothes had dried, the call came for the boy to go out and be "struggled," a common practice against prisoners accused of political infractions. They were returned to their former locales, identified in terms of their political crimes, beaten, and set in the midst of a screaming horde of accusers. The theory behind this action was that the spectacle would provide a lesson to others.

In the vicinity where the street urchin lived, a slogan had been painted on the wall: DOWN WITH IMPERIALISTS! Someone had scraped off the word "Imperialists" and replaced it with "Mao Tse-tung"—an unforgivable anti-government act. The locals accused the boy.

So the morning after he landed in the detention center with Harry, the boy was called out to be mobbed. But his clothes were wet. Harry had worn under his Mao jacket a heavy wool coat of an unauthorized style and color in which he had hoped to escape to Hong Kong. Harry pulled it off and handed it to the boy to wear to his ordeal.

The other men in the cell stared at him. Such a coat for a street urchin?

The boy pulled it on and followed the guard into the corridor. As he passed the other cells, Harry could hear prisoners laughing and jeering.

"Hey, where did this young prince come from?"

Harry had felt sorry for the boy from the moment he entered the prison, filthy, stinking though he was. Harry's heart went out to him because he knew they all agonized together.

Who is high and mighty? he thought. *Who is clean or unclean?* Prison, even before sentencing, became the great leveler where the issues of food and water, a space to sit, and simple survival were the matters of importance. Occupation, education, wealth or poverty held little relevance in the arena into which they had been tossed.

Detention prior to sentencing continued ten months for Harry Lee. During that time the guards brought occasional remittances of money for the Lee family sent from relatives or friends in Hong Kong.

"Sign this," they would order.

Harry signed the first time without comment, authorizing that the checks be cashed. The second time he protested.

"Hey, I hope you take this money to my home. Otherwise my mother and sister will starve," he said.

"You mind your own business. Just put your name to it. Do as you are told."

Much later he discovered that most of the funds never reached his mother. And he never saw his clothes, his wallet, or his glasses again.

"HEY, LEE!" came the order one morning. "Wash up, clean as you can. Put on your best clothes."

Sentencing. The time had come.

Harry had known it was close, because just a few days prior he had been moved from the detention center to another district in Shanghai. He had learned from others congregated in the center that from here they would go for public sentencing.

Another clue was that just before the move he had been photographed. That session had answered some questions he had always wondered about when looking at posters on the streets. Why did people up for sentencing or execution always appear so contrite, so guilty?

When his turn came, Harry learned why.

"Stand over there," the photographer pointed. "No, no! Don't lift your head so high. Look down, look at your knees."

Several guards stood by, guaranteeing cooperation.

"Don't tighten those lips so much," the photographer continued. "Soften your jaw . . . not so grim looking. All right . . . good."

And so, head down, mouth slack and purposeless, Harry learned how the poster pictures were taken.

But in spite of his ten months in detention, his shaven head, the photography session—all the restraints that branded him a criminal—Harry believed in justice. He knew he had committed no crime worthy of death or prison. Now that the time had come for public sentencing, he held out hope that he would be exonerated and set free.

Chapter 8

Handcuffed again, Harry looked up at the people already standing in the back of the big truck. Police with impassive faces stared back, competent professionals accustomed to herding prisoners to and fro; around them swirled Mao's darlings, noisy young Red Guards, chattering to each other as they fastened their scarlet banners to the sides of the truck.

Rough hands boosted Harry and the other captives up beside their guards. *They are the heroes, these red-banded kids,* Harry observed as the motor sputtered to life. *And we are the monsters. We are the counterrevolutionaries with our shaven heads.*

Then his saving streak of humor worked its way to the surface yet again as the truck roared up the street toward the public sentencing event.

Boy, this is grand style, he noted. Heroic stuff. The red flags whipped in the wind. Crowds stood and watched as the Red Guards shouted their slogans and shook their fists at the wintry sky. The irony of prisoners experiencing the same sort of triumphal procession as political leaders or famous athletes held just a moment longer for Harry as he realized they had arrived at the great Shanghai city stadium.

He had come here many times. Here he had watched the Danish badminton team compete against the Chinese. Countless volleyball matches . . . *and now we're going in there*

. . . we're gonna perform. This is our day! The act, the show must go on . . .

Harry jumped down from the truck, and even without his glasses he could tell the stadium was filled with people.

"Uh, Lee . . ."

Harry turned and looked into the face of the man responsible for policing his lane, the cadre who watched over and reported on their neighborhood.

"I don't want you to do anything that wouldn't be good for you," the guard muttered. Harry knew what the man meant. He feared that Harry might behave as some prisoners had done before him during sentencing, screaming out against the system before the crowd. "Down with Communism. Down with Mao!" Venting their anger and despair.

Harry stared at the man for a moment; he knew he was concerned for his former neighbor, but fearful of retaliation should one of his people burst out in public revolt.

Harry raised his hand and gave the cadre a reassuring wave. *No big scenes,* he thought, although he did not speak, *unless we are dealing with big issues. I will save my strength for the time when I must publicly reject my Lord, or die, perhaps, in defense of my faith. That is all that really matters.*

He wondered if the time would come when he would be required to choose, like the early Christians in Nero's amphitheater, to reject the Lord Jesus or die. He had purposed in his heart to be ready for that day, to be strong enough to stand firm in his faith regardless of the pain or disgrace his enemies designed for him. And in the face of this possibility, political outcries and personal rights seemed insignificant indeed.

One by one the manacled prisoners were jerked from the group and swung around to face the judges as the crowd in the stadium watched. Two women came first, two men after them; then the Red Guards dragged Harry forward.

Part of Harry was aware of the searing pain in his twisted,

shackled arms. Part of him wondered if the fairness and justice he had been taught so carefully in school would come into play at this moment.

"The prisoner venomously attacked the various political movements of the great Communist Party in his church services. Further, he betrayed the state and tried to desert to the enemy by seeking to escape. Seven years . . ."

Harry's feet responded automatically to the shoves of the guards who pushed him back among the prisoners, but his mind was flooded with thoughts of acceptance of this shattering moment.

Seven years.

No appeals, he vowed silently.

Harry had seen how a pastor friend's words had been twisted and used against him after he had been dragged off to prison. Huge posters were plastered all over his church charging that "this wicked man stood up in the platform and talked about seed sown in the ground. He said the sun came up and scorched them all to death. That is wicked! Evil! Everybody knows he is pointing a venomous finger at our beloved Chairman Mao. Everybody knows Chairman Mao is called the Sun of the People of China."

Seven years.

"Lord," he prayed, "you work things out for me. I'll not try to do it myself."

It was Christmas Eve 1968.

THAT NIGHT Harry was moved to the Shanghai Municipal Prison, formerly known as Ward Road Prison. Built by the British, it was thought to be one of the largest in Asia. Inmates said that even if you slept in a different cell each night, it would take ten years to use them all.

As Harry and his fellow prisoners were brought up to the three huge gates and watched them swing open to admit the truck in which they were riding, Harry remembered a line of Dante's *Inferno* from his literature class: "All hope abandon, ye who enter here."

Then Harry thought, *I don't ask much. Just let these men leave me alone with my misery for seven years. Throw me into the corner of a cell and there I will stay with my thoughts. That's all I ask.*

The prisoners alighted from the truck. Harry watched the ballet teacher, with whom he had plotted to escape China, bend and offer her back to a crippled woman, a failed suicide. The woman accepted the dancer's help and together they moved slowly up the cement stairs to the women's side of the prison.

Guards led Harry to his cell, a space so narrow he could touch both walls at once by stretching out his arms. A cell built for one man but which he had to share with three others. Because it was impossible for the men to sleep four abreast, they alternated, head to foot, foot to head. A tiny space remained for small clothing bundles and the wooden toilet bucket.

Each newly sentenced prisoner was handed a copy of the accusations against him. Harry read his, the same words spoken against him in the stadium.

That's not true! he fumed. *I never talked about politics in church. I know very well we are to "render to Caesar" what is his. We were an international church. Japanese, American, British, and Germans worshiped with us; even though our countries were at war we had no ill feelings. We were a church! God's people! Harmony and love were our tradition. We were international, interdenominational. We didn't speak against the Communists. We didn't go their way, but we said nothing in church services about this . . . and they accuse us anyway.*

Harry churned these events over in his mind.

Didn't I somehow know this was coming, even while I held onto hope for justice?

He remembered an incident on the train from Canton that had introduced this premonition.

He and Edith still carried with them food they had bought for their boat ride to Hong Kong. Edith did not feel well, however, and had refused the oranges Harry offered her.

"I'd advise you to finish them all," their guard interjected. Harry examined the man's expressionless face. What he had said sounded like a veiled hint that they should enjoy what they could while they could because life for them was going to take a sharp turn for the worse.

But then hard on the heels of Harry's resentment against the unjust accusations came a second reaction.

Well, praise the Lord! I can show this paper to St. Peter at heaven's gate. I can tell him I wasn't sent up for adultery, for embezzlement, for any sin . . . but for serving my Master.

Similar thoughts had stirred his heart with joy during the ordeal with the Red Guards. When they finally left the Lees in peace, Harry knew his tormentors had lost. Yes, they had beaten him, forced him to his knees, humiliated him before his neighbors. But in the face of every evil act, joy sprang up within Harry.

"Lord," he exulted, "this is what they did to you! They spat on you, crowned you with thorns, humiliated you. And I am counted worthy to go through all this? Following in your footsteps? It will be an honor and great glory if I end up in a pool of blood . . . for you!"

So as the other three men in his cell swore through their teeth, tore up their sentences, and threw them into the toilet bucket, Harry gently tucked his into his meager bundle of possessions, not knowing that a time would come when that bit of paper would help to swing open another gate.

*
**

NOW THAT sentencing had taken place and he had been moved from the district detention center to prison, Harry's mother could visit him. They had not seen or communicated with each other for almost a year. And although she had been questioned relentlessly about her son's activities, officials never responded to her pleas for information about him.

Her hair! It's so white! Harry caught his breath at the changes he could see in his mother.

She reached across the table that separated them and gripped his hand. Although Harry had been forbidden to touch his visitors or exchange written messages, he held her hand in his for a few moments before he slowly drew away.

"Did you see my picture on the posters on the walls?" Harry sought to ease the pain with humor. His mother nodded but did not express her feelings at seeing her son accused before all of Shanghai. Only later did he learn from friends that his picture was fourth in a line of twenty on posters prepared before the sentencing session in the stadium and slapped onto the walls throughout the city immediately thereafter.

One of Harry's English students took one down and hid it in his home, thinking to save it until Harry returned. But second thoughts reminded the boy that if his home were searched by Red Guards, such a sentimental gesture could be twisted into accusations with ominous repercussions. So he destroyed it; wisely, too, because the Red Guards did come to call.

Harry's visit from his mother brought him happy news that had been withheld by his captors. Although he had repeatedly asked, "Where is my sister?" no one would tell him her fate, a tactic he was convinced was designed to keep him on edge.

Edith had been released shortly after their arrest in Canton. His pleas for her apparently had been heeded, and although she and her mother underwent questioning and harassment, they remained free.

Harry felt as if he could crawl into the corner of his cell and wait out the seven years, now that his family stood free of prison walls. Dad would be pleased, he felt sure, that his eldest son had cared for them as best he could.

Chapter 9

Harry learned immediately that his desire to sit alone in the corner of his cell was not to be fulfilled. Long hours of quiet reflection had no place on the agenda at Ward Road Prison.

Each morning guards unlocked the cells and, over the echoes of steel bars clanging against masonry walls, shouted the shuffling, sullen men into the corridors for thought reform. "Brainwashing" some call it.

Developed early on by Communist party organizers, thought reform entailed severe regimens, each designed to destabilize the prisoners mentally and emotionally. First, Harry's physical environment was always controlled, along with the information available to him. Officials mixed idealism and terror to achieve their goals; privation, fatigue, and prolonged tension were used to undermine his sense of personal identity. Then repetitive indoctrination sought to replace his shattered ideals with conformity to Communist thought and behavior.

At least that was the plan.

THE INITIAL activity confronting Harry was the matter of writing confessions. "What shall I confess?" he asked. "I've done nothing wrong."

"Write your life story . . . tell everything about yourself . . . all you've done since you were little . . . tell us who your accomplices were . . . make a clean breast of everything."

So Harry wrote. He had quickly learned during the year of detention to adapt whenever possible to the demands of his tormentors. He wrote his life history honestly. He knew, however, that it would not satisfy because he accused no one nor confessed to any crimes against the government.

In the mornings Harry sat against the corridor wall with his cellmates and prisoners from several adjoining cells to study the writings of Marx and Engels. Prisoners were required to confront one another, pointing out where they fell short or resisted the teachings.

Prison food was in short supply. Famine stalked China. Rations for sedentary prisoners, therefore, were cut to the minimum. Every morning food containers were handed through the bars. All they held was congee, a watery porridge with dried or pickled turnips. Later in the day the men received a small amount of rice and vegetables into which they often poured water to create the illusion of full stomachs for a moment or two.

Hungry beyond belief, Harry tried eating toothpaste or ointment. If a bone ever showed up in their food, he and his cellmates crushed it and ate it. The same with egg shells.

Thin and bony, Harry took the two three-inch stacks of toilet paper sheets he had been allotted and used them as a padded seat during the hours of study and struggle he was required to undergo each day. One stack pillowed his head at night.

But the athlete in Harry would not let him wither and quit. As the weeks wore on, his body screamed for activity, for the kind of care he had always given it. The cell was damp; he wanted to avoid problems with arthritis or rheumatism so he began a program of personal calisthenics. During high school Vic, Larry, and he had followed a Charles Atlas body-building course. Harry wondered if he could still do the push-ups. When he suggested the idea, his two younger cellmates wanted to try.

"Move back. Make room and let's see what I can do."

"Huh, with the amount of food they give us, it's a wonder we can still walk."

". . . five, six, seven . . ." His spindly arms trembling from the effort, the first fellow collapsed on the floor.

"Let me try. How does it work?" The other cellmate had never seen push-ups. Harry explained, but this one could not clear the floor even once.

Harry's turn. Memories of happier days came flooding back. Days when three energetic, idealistic boys read the direction book, then set to work developing, strengthening, and honing their bodies for the simple joy of knowing they were in superb condition.

". . . seventeen, eighteen, nineteen . . ." Harry's arms pumped up and down, moving the straight line of his body with them.

". . . thirty-five, -six, -seven, -eight . . ." The other three men grew silent, watching Harry with impassive faces. How far could he go?

Fifty push-ups had always been the goal of the Three Musketeers. *Can I still make it?* Harry wondered as his pace slowed. But one at a time he wrung still more push-ups from his protesting body.

". . . forty-eight . . . for-ty-nine . . . a-a-and fifty!" Unable to help themselves, Harry's cellmates cheered as he dropped face down onto the floor, his ribcage heaving.

As he waited for his breathing to calm and his heart to quit racing, Harry felt deep pleasure. *I can still do it, even after all this,* he congratulated himself.

Push-ups were not the only discipline practiced by this tough and wiry child of God. Morning washups in winter were a grim prospect for the inmates of Ward Road Prison. The windows stayed open all night and the weather grew so cold that the towels left to dry on the cell crossbars froze by morning.

So when water, apportioned the evening before and kept in basins outside the cells, was ladled out in the morning, most of the prisoners turned away from it and huddled in their thick, padded coats, indifferent to personal hygiene. Cleanliness came at too high a price. Who cared anyway?

Harry cared. Harry and one other man in his cell. Lice and other vermin awaited those who did not care and so the two of them crawled from their warm bedrolls each winter morning before the whistle blew, and stripped and washed in the icy water.

Harry looked at the other man. "Steam," he said.

"What?"

"Steam is rising from your shoulders."

"Yours, too."

Harry dumped the remaining cold water on his shaven head. It was impossible to tell for an instant if he were scalding or freezing. Then he could feel the blood pumping, pulsing through his head, his steaming shoulders, his arms, legs, and feet. It was glorious! Like icy rain on his face in the morning. Like the sea wind reddening his ears on the front of the Shanghai trams. Harsh, invigorating, bearable. And best of all, he was clean!

WITHIN MONTHS of his sentencing, a collection of difficulties clustered around Harry Lee that made hunger, cold, and lack of space seem like a celebration.

One morning the guards opened cells at the usual study time, but instead of ordering the prisoners to sit in the corridor outside their doors, they herded them into a larger space where they sat in a circle.

"All right, Lee," a guard growled at Harry. "Come to the middle here and start confessing."

Harry stared back at him, blank and confused. "Confess? Confess what?"

"Don't look so innocent. Make a clean breast of it."

Harry did not know what was happening. Oh, he knew that prisoners tried to communicate with each other and he knew that someone always told on them. The system of accusation and reward was carefully nurtured by the authorities, but he knew he had had no part of their sinister activities.

Guilty or not, however, here Harry stood again in a circle of accusers and had to protest his innocence against their shouts. Then as he fell silent and listened to their charges, he understood how his actions had hurled him into this disaster. It all began with a young man's question:

"Will you teach me some English?"

He wanted to learn something to help while away the years, this fellow victim of madness called the Cultural Revolution. The guards sneeringly called him "Little Chiang." He bore the unforgivable taint of a distant relationship to the hated Nationalist leader, Chiang Kai-shek. Swept into prison with thousands of others accused of dissatisfaction with the government, the young man saw his dream of medical school evaporate.

So Harry Lee, intimate with the pain of lost dreams, accepted the scraps of paper Little Chiang passed from the next cell. On them he had written anatomical and medical terms in Chinese; Harry wrote the English words beside them and passed the paper back. When they ran out of medical terms, it was sports, music—whatever interested Little Chiang. Together they compiled a pathetic little dictionary on grimy bits of paper.

But now those innocent exercises, those meager flights of freedom, were being twisted into acts of anti-state hostility. Guards and prison officials were convinced that a major insurrection simmered among their inmates. They set cellmates against each other, encouraging clandestine reports and accusations. Harry was caught in the crossfire.

Little Chiang was accused of leading a plot to overthrow prison authority and take possession of the weapons arsenal. Because of his family ties to the Nationalists and his desperate cries against the injustice of a system that refused him education, he of course would be guilty as accused.

". . . and you, Lee, you are his lackey. You passed secret coded messages back and forth with him that nobody could understand . . . he wants you for his foreign minister, doesn't he, when you overthrow the government? . . . we know all about it . . ."

At the same time Harry learned that the man he secretly labeled "a lovable pickpocket" was accused of being chosen as finance minister, assuming he would use his acquisitive talents to raise and control the funds of the new government. And the boxer-wrestler in a cell further down the corridor was to be defense minister.

Great material for comedy if the accusations had been confined to a book or a movie. But the screaming mouths, the kicks and blows were deadly serious—with more to come.

The guard walked up to Harry, who was still standing within the circle of his accusers, and held out a pair of handcuffs.

Sharp memories flashed through Harry's mind as he put his hands behind his back. He had seen men spread-eagled on the bars, held there by these steel circles. He had watched more than once when tough young men writhed and screamed as soon as their arms were twisted back and caught into what they grimly called "the jet plane position." Now it was his turn. The guard clicked the handcuffs behind Harry's back—not on his wrists, but up on his forearms. Pain tore through Harry like a white hot fire. He grimaced and contorted his body, trying to ease its torture.

"I really don't know anything . . . don't know what you're asking me . . . let me go, please . . ." He pleaded with the man who held the key.

"Confess! Confess!" was all the guard would say. He betrayed not so much as a flicker of concern over Harry's agony. Then Harry silently made a choice: *All right. From now on I know I can look to man no longer. The only thing to do is look to my Lord.*

From that moment on, Harry said nothing even though the searing anguish from the steel bands around his arms kept him writhing.

Harry's tormentor was confused. Never had a man been able to withstand such torture before. Within seconds his victims always spewed out all sorts of confession about their own misdeeds plus everything they knew about the activities of their associates or accomplices.

But this small, strong person had nothing to say, in spite of the blinding pain. The guard watched him through narrowed eyes, listening at the same time to the changing cadence of the other prisoners' comments.

Their initial, obligatory accusations were melting into murmurs of sympathy and admiration. They had never seen a man endure the handcuffs for so long!

Sensing that his advantage was dissolving, the guard grabbed Harry and dragged him back toward his cell. Harry muttered through his anguish. "I don't know anything . . . I don't know anything . . ."

The guard threw Harry into the cell, handcuffs still clamped around his throbbing arms. Harry staggered across the tiny room and crumpled against the wall. Perspiration poured down his face. Eyes closed, teeth clenched against the agony that racked him, he understood at that moment why men eagerly killed themselves here. A leap from that window would bring blessed release. To knot a towel around your neck and dangle off into death, a sweet comfort. Other men did it all the time. They even took the long needles issued to resew their padded bedding and drove them into their hearts.

For a man with no hope, it was the only answer.

*
**

ABOUT FORTY-FIVE minutes later, the guard came back to Harry's cell expecting to hear a blithering, broken man plead for release. Instead he found a silent, twisted form leaning in a corner and drenched in sweat, eyes closed, mouth drawn and grim with pain.

"Oh, dozing, eh?" he said. "Taking it easy, are you?"

He jerked Harry from the comfort of the wall, took out his key—and tightened the cuffs, like dragon's claws, another notch, crushing the steel deeper into the flesh of Harry's arms. At the onset of fresh pain, the tortured prisoner teetered on the brink of unconsciousness.

The guard then shoved Harry back toward his corner. Sweat gushed again from Harry's pores. He felt as if death were pulling him close.

Just then the other three prisoners in Harry's cell were returned for the day. They had their instructions.

"Hey, Lee," one said. "Don't be so stubborn! Hurry up and confess! Say you'll talk, and he'll take off those handcuffs. Promise to write up everything, then you'll be all right."

"I don't know what he wants me to tell," Harry rasped through clenched teeth. "Who am I to accuse? . . . I can't make up a story . . . I can't save my skin with false accusations . . . later on I'd only be in more trouble. . . ."

Harry found that he could take anything rather than break God's laws on truth, integrity, and honesty. These qualities mystified the men in his cell.

"If you're going to be so stubborn, you will lose your

arms," they warned. "Leave those cuffs on long enough, without blood circulating—it's dangerous!"

At that Harry's mind journeyed back to boyhood reading about tourniquets. You twisted one on, he knew, to stop blood flowing from a wound or to localize poison from snakebite. But it must be loosened every twenty minutes. Otherwise the leg or arm would wither away with no blood to feed it.

I am going to lose my two arms, he thought. *No writing, no drawing . . . how awful! These two hands are so precious, so useful . . . what will I do?"*

The day wore on, an interminable sentence. The bedtime whistle finally blew, and Harry's three cellmates crawled into their bedrolls. He slouched against the wall, unable to sit or lie down, drenched with sweat and pale as death. His arms remained twisted behind him, his shoulders hunched forward with the strain. Numbness eased the anguish at last; Harry took it as a gift from God.

MIDNIGHT. A change of guards. The new one began his duty by peering into cell number 23.

"Hey, Lee. You gonna confess?"

"I don't know what to talk about. It's my same old story. I'm a greenhorn here . . . never been to prison before. I don't know your ways. What am I supposed to do? I tell only the truth."

The other men awoke as soon as the guard approached. They tried again to fulfill their assignment to persuade Harry to talk.

"Come on, man. It's your last chance. Say you'll confess and tomorrow morning you'll write it. Get those handcuffs off . . . then you can lie down and sleep . . . and you'll still have your arms."

"I don't know what to talk about."

The guard sighed with exasperation. "Look," he said. "I'm gonna let you go, but tomorrow you write that confession or else . . ."

Harry did not speak, but through the haze of pain he thought, *Yes, you are letting me go . . . but tomorrow we start all over again."*

The guard, standing in the corridor, told Harry to back up to the bars. He put the key into the handcuff lock and turned it. The cuffs had to be pulled away from Harry's upper arms. The steel had long since clawed through the skin and into his flesh. Blood poured from the wound in his right arm.

Again, God's gift of numbness. Harry collapsed into his small space on the floor and into oblivion.

Chapter 10

Harry's strength and endurance became the talk of Ward Road Prison. They evoked opposing reactions within the walls: one was admiration laced with fear; the other, antagonism and determination to bring that Lee fellow to his emotional and physical knees.

Prison officials tried several tactics. They changed the other men in cell 23, introducing three tough, young hooligans who had been told of Harry's courage and were instructed to wear him down.

Harry was hauled up daily to be mobbed by the other prisoners. Before they began, the guard would jerk him to his feet and coach the others. "Don't pity this man. He looks old, he's frail and small, and he wears glasses; so meek and mild, he seems. Put the heat to him. He can stand it."

Everyone in the prison knew that Harry Lee, although more than forty years old, held the endurance record with handcuffs. The guard added to their information about the small, calm man who stood in their midst: "He can do fifty push-ups in his cell. He washes his body with ice water in winter. You can see how these counterrevolutionaries of the underground group are toughening themselves, getting ready for that day when they escape, seize the armory, kill the guards, and overturn the government."

Former cellmates would chime in. "Yeah, when I slept next to him, in the middle of the night I could feel him kicking . . . doing kung fu exercises in his bedroll . . . special breathing, too."

Harry was regularly dragged from sleep for midnight questionings. The guards' remarks revealed their surprise at his ability to rest in spite of all their carefully plotted pressures. Other prisoners, haunted by the specter of torture past and future, never slept so soundly.

Another questioning technique boomeranged on the authorities and aided the tough little man who would not break. After interrogation sessions, guards occasionally offered their victim an extra canteen of rice. They thought that men who were trying to hide guilt live in fear of discovery; so when such prisoners were offered an extra portion of food, inner turmoil would theoretically prevent them from eating it.

Not Harry. Whenever he was confronted by this devious test, he eagerly took up his chopsticks and devoured whatever food they gave him while guards stood by, waiting in vain for him to turn sick with apprehension.

MEANWHILE, Harry did not fare so well at the hands of his new cellmates, who zealously worked at extracting confession from him. At first they kicked him whenever he dozed in the daytime after a night's interrogation.

"Asleep, huh?" one would growl at him. "If you want to sleep, you confess."

But when a mere kick to the jaw failed to make him grovel, Harry was forced to undergo new agonies.

"All right, Lee, stand up!" they would say. "Get to the corner . . . you gonna confess?"

Harry eyed his tormentors from the corner and knew in his heart that they halfway feared him. They had looked him over carefully when they first entered cell 23. He heard them mutter that he looked like a Japanese boxer. So the three of them always worked together, even though he never menaced them in any way.

"What am I to confess? I told everything."

"All right, then, Lee, . . . ninety degrees."

"Ninety degrees" was a technique prescribed to Harry's cellmates by the guards, who instructed them, "Squeeze it out of him quick." It meant he was to bend forward from his waist until his torso was parallel with the floor. After being in this position for a while, Harry's head began to swim. A few minutes later, pain invaded his back. He moved tentatively to one side then the other, seeking relief.

"You move, huh?" One of the men came at him with a vicious kick that sent Harry sprawling into the opposite corner of the cell. Lights and pain exploded like fireworks inside his head as they continued to beat him.

"Ninety degrees, Lee!" Harry hauled himself erect again, then bent to the required angle. One of the men lounged against the wall nearby until Harry was absorbed into his private world of pain, then he swung his fist at Harry's bent back, delivering kidney punches that made the pain in his spine seem insignificant.

From the morning whistle until the night whistle they kept at him. Several days were consumed in this crucible of humiliation and pain. His only moments of release came at mealtime, when the men allowed Harry to sit and eat.

But then, "Hurry up . . . hurry up! Finished? All right, get to the position again."

"I can't bear this," he whispered.

"Oh, can't you? Then you can write. Otherwise, keep the position."

Just at the point where Harry Lee thought his back would break from the strain, just when he began to believe that suicide would be a welcome release, his Comforter intervened once again. Harry discovered a way out.

Every time he raised his head even slightly, Harry's three tormentors battered him with blows. But if he bent lower, they ignored him. He turned this discovery over in his mind.

"Perhaps they think I'm seeking pity by bending lower, so they don't pay any attention then . . . and it does ease things a bit . . . let's see if it works . . ."

Again Harry's physical resilience served him well. Part of the fitness program of the Three Musketeers had been backbends over a piano stool, so his back muscles were strong and well developed. Bending so low that his nose neared his kneecaps actually brought the suffering man a modicum of relief from the strain of the agonizing ninety-degree angle.

Always testing the attitudes of those around him, Harry concluded that when he bent lower, his tormentors felt he was playing on their sympathies, so they ignored him. Looking at his contorted body, they believed it must hurt more when he bent lower.

Harry used this misunderstanding and groaned and sighed as he bent forward further than the required ninety degrees.

"Ah, leave him alone," one said with a grin. The others agreed that their victim was obviously suffering great pain— but Harry was practicing the only method available to him to ease the agony.

SOLITARY CONFINEMENT. Isolation. No showers with other prisoners. Beatings, torture, ridicule, and slander. No family visits. What was next? Execution?

Death always lurked close by, Harry knew. Prisoners regularly killed themselves in a variety of grisly ways. He had no guarantee that his forty-year-old body would continue to survive the torture and deprivation. Would he retain his sanity in this narrow world of hate and bigotry, he who had grown up in an environment of beauty and goodness? He had seen other inmates of Ward Road Prison screaming out their private agonies, raging against their circumstances, pushed beyond the limits of sanity.

Possessed of a deep confidence in God, Harry could not help but ask some elemental questions: Am I God's? Am I born again? Without a doubt a Christian?

Prayer had always been his practice, conversations with God his meat and drink. Having to give up his customary prayer posture of kneeling beside his bed, Harry had found that talking with the Lord could be done in any place or position. At night he prayed flat on his back after the whistle blew. At first he hoped God was not offended by his disrespectful stance, but then he came to enjoy knowing that he was looking straight into the face of his Creator. The love bonds strengthened between them, and Harry never missed his nightly encounter with the Lord.

He prayed for Nadia as he had done since she left China. Those moments of intercession for his sweetheart deepened the sense of loss he felt at not hearing from her—her letters stopped coming during the Cultural Revolution. But he never stopped praying for her. And he never stopped loving her.

Harry sometimes thought of Nadia's offer to send money to him and his family from her home in Australia. He had written back suggesting that she save it there; perhaps they would need it more when he got out of China some day.

But would he ever leave China? Would he ever see Nadia again? Did she know where he was now?

During the Cultural Revolution, only Miss Elizabeth Ward, his former Sunday school teacher, was able to send mail to him in Shanghai from Hong Kong. She had told him that she sent copies of his letters to his scattered friends from the Endeavourers Church. So perhaps Nadia knew.

*
* *

IN SPITE OF regular prayer and the steady supply of Scripture drawn from memory that sustained his mind and heart, Harry struggled with despair as he watched the city dust creep in around the window in his cell.

"Why am I having to waste these years, my best years, Lord?" he cried, "All I want is to serve you."

Why should Larry and Vic live in freedom, raise families, pursue careers? Why should all their dreams come true while his did not? After all, his greatest hope was to obey God's call into the ministry. It wasn't as if he wanted to accumulate money or make the Lee name famous.

"God, I just wanted to train to work for you—to lead my church, to preach, to teach. Why is this happening to me? Don't I deserve better since I promised to obey you? Why, God, why?"

With scarred arms, damaged kidneys, and an aching spine, Harry lay on his back in the tiny space allotted him in cell 23 and counted yet again the eight steel bars that held him prisoner. His battered body and the turmoil of unanswered questions seemed all of a piece. But out beyond the bars in the blue velvet sky shone a star. Harry gazed at the pinpoint of light and found himself remembering a conversation between Jesus and His disciple, Peter. The story appeared in the twenty-first chapter of the gospel of John. He'd read it countless times, this story of Jesus' third encounter with a few of His disciples after His resurrection.

Jesus and Peter conversed about his future, and Peter, so utterly human, pointed his finger at John and said, "What about him, Lord? What's going to happen to him?"

Jesus' reply to His pupil repeated itself over and over in Harry's brain: "What is that to thee? Follow thou me."

Never mind Larry and Vic. Don't worry about seminary. Trust Me with your abused body, your breaking heart. You follow Me; I am your Lord. I have not stopped loving you. You are mine and I am here with you.

The pinprick of starlight seemed to flood the cell. Great peace enveloped Harry and protected him, body, mind, and soul. His questions turned to affirmations.

"Lord, as long as it is for your honor and glory, it is all right with me. Larry has gone one way, Vic another . . . and I am here. I say 'amen' to it. I trust you, Jesus."

Harry pondered the scene on the beach. Jesus stood flanked by Peter and John. "Lord, what you've just said sounds as if John's going to live to a ripe old age," Peter might have protested. "It sounds as if I'm headed for something violent and short. Lord, is that fair?"

But then Harry imagined Peter having second thoughts.

"It doesn't matter, Lord. As long as it is for your honor and glory . . . whether by life or by death . . . it will be all right."

After all, Harry mused, *Peter couldn't know that John had to live long enough to write the Book of Revelation from his lonely Aegean island.*

"For your honor and glory, Lord. Larry has his life, Vic his . . . happy with their families and careers . . . and I am here.

"Amen, Father. So be it."

Harry's whys turned to miraculous joy even though he had not gained one ounce of additional understanding. He had gained great faith, however—bullheaded, stiff-necked, stubborn faith.

"Prove Me now," God seemed to be saying to Harry Lee. From that time on, cell 23 could not hold him. Even during the weeks of struggles and questioning, occasional quiet moments did come. And when they did, his mind soared on the wings of Scripture he had learned. Memories of church-centered events came tumbling back complete with the warmth, the joy, the rightness of it all. Loving relationships still warmed him . . . Granny, Dad, his fellow Musketeers,

Miss Ward, Nadia. Beyond the eight bars a sparrow chirped or a star shone, and through them God spoke.

There were still times when Harry felt as if his life was dribbling away day by precious day. He still mourned that he would never receive training for the ministry he hungered to fulfill. But with these thoughts came Job's declaration: "Though he slay me, yet will I trust in him" (Job 13:15).

The inability to understand the inscrutable ways of God no longer bothered Harry. Belonging to Him was enough. Harry kept his hand in the Master's, for he knew this was his only refuge.

Harry Lee on Easter Sunday 1954; Harry's Sunday school teacher and benefactor, Elizabeth Ward

"The Three Musketeers" in 1943 (from left), Harry, Vic Carlsen, and Larry Klyhn

Dick and Jean Hassall, OMS missionaries, and their children, in whose home Harry was converted to Christianity

Dr. Henry G. C. Hallock, who founded the Endeavourers Church

Harry giving the first reading at the Christmas Eve service in the
Holy Trinity Cathedral, Shanghai, in 1957

Missionaries Larry Klyhn (above left) and Ed Kilbourne, son of "Uncle Bud" Kilbourne, in 1981; (left) Harry on his seminary graduation day

Harry honored at his graduation from Western Evangelical
Seminary, Portland, Oregon, on May 25, 1984

Chapter 11

The weeks dragged on within Ward Road Prison's massive walls. Harry Lee and his fellow inmates knew nothing of events in China, let alone the world beyond. The perimeters of their existence extended only from accusation to struggle to beatings. Whistles and shouts and kicks controlled their activities, which were limited to waking, washing, eating, working, studying Mao thought, and sleeping.

Harry knew that according to the law he had begun to serve his sentence when he was first detained in Canton and that it continued through the months he served in Shanghai prior to public sentencing. Time was winding down at last. On the day when his seven years were finally up, he believed, he would walk free again.

Harry did not know that the Cultural Revolution had sputtered out, that thousands of red-banded youth had been scattered throughout the nation's remote areas for labor and rehabilitation. He could have predicted that their brand of radicalism would shred government structure and Communist party loyalties, even though information about this turmoil never leaked through his prison bars.

He did not know that border disputes between China and Russia were heating to the boiling point, that troops were massing along the frontiers even as leaders sought noncombative ways to defuse the volatile situation.

Most remarkable of all, along with Harry Lee, few inhabitants of the free world knew that the American secretary of state, Henry Kissinger, was moving slowly and delicately toward conversation with his Chinese counterpart—these two men representing a pair of giant nations who had turned their backs on one another in hostility since 1949.

In 1971, long before Harry could hope for release, China had begun to reach out, groping toward diplomatic ties with the rest of the world. These tentative efforts set in motion a remarkable series of events that would miraculously affect the remainder of his life and the ministry he yearned for.

Talks between Kissinger and Chinese Premier Chou Enlai resulted in a visit to China from President Richard Nixon, an event that held Americans transfixed before their television sets. News of this astounding occurrence seeped into Ward Road Prison. Guards lectured prisoners on what their attitudes and behavior should be in the face of the visit of this capitalistic leader. Harry and his fellow inmates would never so much as see a photograph of Nixon, but even so, his coming to China afforded prison officials an opportunity to be sure their charges had their ideologies straight.

Harry began to notice attitudes easing among prison guards. Their witch-hunt had not unearthed the secret, underground counterrevolutionary group they claimed was hidden in the prison. Questionings and torture abated. Their paranoia and fear of political conspiracy died. Harry did his part by seeking to please his captors and allay their fears whenever possible. Even though he could not confess to nonexistent plots, he looked for ways to say something positive and true about the government.

"Chinese athletes are improving rapidly under the socialist system," he wrote. "When I was in school and running relay races, I was considered good, but the records we established then can now be broken by many of today's girls!"

This pleased the guards so much that one of the sports-loving ones decided to organize a relay race among the prisoners. Harry chuckled at the spectacle of himself and the others stumbling around the exercise yard stiff, emaciated, and weak. But his commitment to fitness provided him with the shred of strength he needed to outrun—or outstumble—his fellow prisoners. When he puffed across the finish line ahead of the competition, the organizing guard looked pleased indeed. The man who complimented the government on encouraging athletics was an athlete himself.

Even in this wretched prison, in spite of suspicion and hostility fostered by the system, tenuous bonds of mutual regard reached across the chasm between Communist and Christian. God's keeping power enabled Harry to see his tormentors as people. And though forbidden to share his faith with them, he could watch their eyes and respond to the curiosity or the humor he found there.

The chief guard on his floor knew of Harry's love for sports. "Bring out the net for volleyball, Lee," he would call, and then wait for Harry's eyes to light up. Harry knew the man liked to please him; perhaps in another place, at another time, they could have been friends.

Returning one day from a rare exercise period, Harry, jacket slung over his shoulder and sweat glistening on his face, encountered a young woman officer fresh from police college. Her eyes widened in pity and sympathy at the sight of him.

She's new . . . she doesn't think I look like a criminal. Harry's sensitivity told him much about the young woman. *She expected rapists and robbers. She didn't expect to find civilized, ordinary people, even people who wear glasses. How long before she acquires a wooden face like the others, before she loses her humanity?*

He shuddered at the horror that had mutilated his homeland as the guards locked him back into his cell.

*
**

IN THE SPRING of 1975, Harry Lee knew his seven-year ordeal was ending. Even though pressures had eased and his body had begun to heal, he didn't dwell on this mending, this precious gift of relief. Instead, anticipation of release from prison consumed his thoughts, crowding out every other benefit he experienced. Men whose sentences coincided knew each other, and those whose time was finishing murmured together about the future, the freedom they longed for.

Sure enough, one day Harry was moved to another section of the prison along with about fifty others whose terms resembled his. Here they listened again to interminable harangues about becoming useful members of society. He knew that prison officials also were taking this opportunity to observe their behavior and thought processes one more time, to determine if they were ready for release.

But with senses sharpened by seven years of testing the attitudes and behavior of those around him, Harry suspected that all was not going well. The look on the guards' faces. Not-so-coincidental comments during study group sessions. Then the blunt and bitter truth:

"Brainwashing has not been effective. You are going to the prison farm."

Harry's captors pronounced his continuing doom one morning when all the fifty men in his group were called out and divided into two sections. Harry's heart froze in his chest. His dreams disintegrated.

Prison farm. If you're sent to the prison farm, they transfer your legal residence from home to farm. Such a transfer slams shut the final gate behind you. You don't belong somewhere else any more. You will never return home now. That paper says this is your home, so why should they allow you to go anywhere else?

But one small bright star still shone in Harry Lee's sky. He found even in this bitterest of blows a cause for gratitude.

"Well, Lord, I didn't want to die where there is only steel and concrete. If I am to die, let it be where I can see trees and blue sky, where I can hear birds sing."

The knowledge that he would be close to natural things created by God helped to ease the realization that the Chinese government did not trust him. They believed him to be a counterrevolutionary and therefore more dangerous than ordinary felons. Justice played no part in his transfer to the prison farm; if the justice he had learned about as a schoolboy existed now, he would have been going back to Shanghai.

But hope refused to die. God's miracle peace guarded Harry as he accepted the two loaves of bread handed him as he was herded onto the bus waiting in the prison courtyard. Heavily staffed with guards, the bus left before dawn for Anhui Province, rumbling westward for several hours beneath a dark, dismal sky. Caps were forbidden, and the prisoners' shaved heads guaranteed easy identification should they escape.

After roll call at the prison farm, Harry discovered that he would sleep in a bunk in the large common room into which they were herded.

A bed? After seven years of sleeping on floors? What luxury! he mused. He discovered his mattress was made of sorghum canes. *Just like a Simmons!*

His comment was not sarcasm. The space, natural materials, fresh air, and the rustle of husks were far better than the cold damp of hard gray walls.

Newcomers began by reporting their thoughts, mind control being the trademark of the Communist government. "I am glad I see mountains and streams," Harry told them. "We have a beautiful country here."

And since he felt this would be his final earthly home, he continued, "I am going to put all my efforts into building our country. Since I am a prisoner and have sinned against the people, I am going to make up for all that. I will sweat and through labor reform myself."

Labor he did. Assigned to the vegetable fields later on, Harry worked each day through the spring and on into the summer. Stripped to the waist in the broiling sun, he dug and hoed and lifted until sweat rolled down his back and dripped from his chin. But when he stopped to dry his face, he could look toward the hills and see wild azaleas blooming there.

Flowers! How wonderful! This is God's country . . . and He loves me!

The place was lovely to him, even though he expected to live out his days raising cabbages and responding to roll call. To breathe fresh air, to be out of the confining cell and away from the sordidness of Ward Road Prison lifted his heart and enabled him to praise his Lord.

At first he had wondered if he would survive the physical activity now demanded of him. Seven cramped, sedentary years without proper food had left Harry weak and emaciated in spite of his superior fitness. Guards at the prison farm faced this problem with every new group of arrivals; they tested each prisoner for physical strength.

The first thing Harry had to do was pick up a pole and balance pails of water suspended from either end. Even young men staggered under this typical peasant's load. Along with years of inactivity and inadequate food was the prisoners' unfamiliarity with this kind of work. Harry could not even get the buckets to clear the ground.

Maybe my old cellmates were right, he thought. When he had talked about dying where there are trees and fields, they scoffed. "You want to go to the prison farm? We'd rather stay here. You'll be worked to death over there."

Harry could not even stand with the pole and pails. How could he work all day? And since he couldn't, would he face punishment and death by flogging?

Next morning the guards hustled the newcomers outside and set them running around the mountains. Some fainted along the way. Harry found that his extraordinary supply of strength was gone, his breath and energy exhausted within minutes. But the guards kept pushing the men, anticipating that exercise and increased rice rations would transform these skeletons into farm workers.

It did. Once Harry's lungs were restored to capacity and his joints working smoothly, the guards assigned him to carry pig manure across long fields. By the end of the summer he overheard the commandant mutter to a guard, "Yes, even this Lee is coming along now."

As the weeks wore on, Harry learned why the guards had worked so hard to build up the prisoners. The business of growing vegetables for the prison farm and for the troops who passed through the area was not for weaklings. Harry determined that his representation of Christianity would honor the One he served. Although he was middle-aged, he would work as hard and do as well as any man there.

There were days when, as large drops of rain began to fall, he and his vegetable team would be ordered out to help other teams bundle and bring in the grain drying in the fields before the rain ruined it. As he and the others slaved and slithered in the mud, struggling to move huge loads of grain, Harry would mutter through his clenched teeth.

"I can do it. I don't need pity and I don't need help . . . I can do it."

WINTER BROUGHT other challenges. On rainy days the men made rope from straw, rolling the strands between their palms—rope used to tie plants to stakes and to package the produce. When rains held off, they dug the fertile silt from river bottoms and carried it to the fields to improve soil quality even when the rivers were half frozen. Often they worked extra hours at night by lantern light. They rebuilt dikes around rice paddies and reworked drainage patterns, always driven to produce more food and to improve the yield of their acres.

Harry still had no Bible to read, nor could he kneel by his bunk to pray. Someone reported him for bowing his head to say thanks before eating his meal one day, and Harry was called to stand before the commandant.

"In this place we do not allow propagation of religion in any form," the commandant growled. "Do not let this happen again. I think you know what we do to prisoners who break rules and regulations."

Rather than face a flogging while suspended from the rafters, Harry gave up saying grace in the traditional way. Instead, after picking up his meal from the window at the prisoners' mess, as he walked across the courtyard he turned his face up and thanked his Lord for food. Then when he sat in his place with the other men, he ate as they did and hoped his tormentors considered him reformed. He and other Christians husbanded their strength for the time when they would be forced to deny their Lord. Then they expected to make a stand.

It frustrated Harry not to be allowed to sing. Even after torture back in the Shanghai prison, his body covered with bruises and marks, from somewhere inside the songs came welling up, songs of praise to God. But under prison rules, his Christian music would be interpreted as an effort to proselytize. No praying, no singing, no Bible reading.

An innovative solution came to Harry one day as he listened to the Communist indoctrination songs blaring from the loudspeakers. The words were blurred beyond comprehension as the corridors reverberated with the sound, but he thought the stirring, martial tempo resembled "Onward Christian Soldiers" or "The Battle Hymn of the Republic."

I'll use their tunes to sing my Lord's praise, he decided. *I don't know the words anyway, so I'll sing along with la-la-la.*

As he raised his voice in improvised song, the focus of his mind and heart centered on his soldiering for Jesus Christ, standing firm, singing in the dark night like Paul and Silas. Harry's spirits always lifted and a grin broke forth whenever he honored the Lord with Communist music. Other prisoners looked at him askance.

"Has he lost his mind? Converted to Communism?"

As he searched for morsels to feed his soul, Harry's body remained hungry all the time. He dreamed of food as he slept. Although food here was better than in Ward Road Prison, he worked much harder, burning up the calories that still proved inadequate for good health.

On Chinese New Year's Eve the men were given a special treat to keep them from contemplating escape or suicide. Instead of the usual four or five dishes to choose from and buy, they read a list of thirty-five or forty items of meat, fish, poultry, and vegetables.

Where did all this bounty come from? The old dogs had been killed, and their young had taken their places to watch the prison farm. (A similar fate awaited these.) The old buffalo, no longer fit to plow, was butchered. The pond was dragged for fish. Farmers brought their chickens and ducks for this most important of all Chinese holidays.

Harry held out his container to the men with ladles.

"Give me one of each dish on the blackboard." He gestured toward the chalk-written list of food. "Put the wet stuff at the bottom, the dry stuff on the top."

The men behind the counter grinned. Here was one fellow who was going to enjoy his holiday to the full. Harry took his metal pot brimming with food and returned to the side of his bunk. He pulled out the low bamboo stool and sat down, chopsticks in hand.

Would all this food push from his mind the painful

memories of New Year's excitement at home in Shanghai? He knew his family would be polishing windows, buying special things for the holiday, cooking, preparing. Well, he was buying special things, too, and here they all were before him, steaming and fragrant and ready to eat.

Harry sat alone. Prisoners were allowed to buy a bottle of beer each for the holiday, but he chose not to do so. For two and a half hours he ate, slowly biting and chewing and swallowing until he had finished the whole pot of food. He had spent the pittance earned by his labor in the vegetable fields on a huge meal. He relished every morsel.

AND SO THE SMALL JOYS gained weight somehow and created a balance against the awful reality of imprisonment for Harry Lee. His tough, tenacious spirit hung on, and beyond grit-toothed survival it found hope to go along with each new sunrise.

"Expect the best; be prepared for the worst" was the philosophy he developed. When other men on the prison farm told of their long, toil-filled terms, of their forgotten status, half of his heart said, "This is what will happen to me. Let's settle down, now. No false hopes."

But the other half replied, "Nothing is impossible for my Lord. And Father, if you'll open the way, I am still your servant and I still want to go to seminary. Let your will be done and your name glorified."

Resignation versus refusal to give up. Harry decided that to be like a cork in troubled waters was the answer; accept being pulled under when strong forces prevailed. But as soon as the adversaries gave up, he could bob up again into the brightness of God's blessing and love.

Chapter 12

Harry huddled against the cold December wind and thrust his hands deeper into the sleeves of his padded coat. He peered at the long grass around his feet, thankful for the heavy boots that protected him from snakes. Many times in the past three years he had pulled guard duty in the vegetable fields, so the hillside graves were like old friends welcoming him when he settled his small wooden stool among them and began his vigil.

Huge white radishes and tall cabbages remained in the field. Harry and his teammates had to watch them each night, because hungry villagers would steal them if they could.

"What a night!" he murmured. The moon stood just behind his shoulder and stars spangled the great dark bowl of the sky. As he turned over his memories one by one and talked with his heavenly Father, one thought jolted him upright.

"Why, it's almost Christmas!" he said. "Jesus was born on such a night as this ... and here I sit like the shepherds. Only I'm not watching sheep, I'm guarding cabbages."

Delighted with his discovery and with his sense of participation in Jesus' coming, Harry longed to sing Christmas carols, to throw his head back and express his praise and joy through the songs he learned as a boy.

Men and women all over the world who love the Christ are preparing to celebrate His birth ... the shops are full of good things . . . women are baking and cooking for those they love. I imagine anywhere you turn the radio dial you can hear Christmas music. I want to join in, to be part of it with them!

Harry's thoughts raced and his heartbeat quickened as his imagination painted in vivid colors, scents, and sounds the activities that set the rest of the world awhirl.

But this was a prison farm. A Communist prison farm. He had already suffered reprimands and torture because of his devotion to this Son of God. The wind was blowing back toward the settlement from Harry's post overlooking the fields. Should he sing, the men would hear him.

He wet his finger and held it up in the wind. No doubt about it, it was blowing straight toward the barracks.

"Ah, Lord, you know how full is my heart. And I can't even give you a few carols for your birthday."

He moistened his finger again, but detected no change. He hoped no one would try to steal anything tonight—how hard it would be to drive them away, still hungry, when God sent His Son so they might live!

Then a sense of change disturbed Harry's thoughts. Was the grass bending the other way? Could he hear more clearly the yells of the gamblers back in the common room?

Harry licked his finger one more time and held it high above his head. No question, the wind had shifted. Now it cooled the back of his neck whereas before it had blown into his face.

While shepherds watched their flocks by night,
All seated on the ground . . .

Harry straightened his thin shoulders inside his heavy jacket, placed a hand on either knee, and began to sing.

The angel of the Lord came down,
And glory shone around,
And glory shone around.

One after another Harry sang the old and lovely songs that celebrate God's love for His world, that tell how His only Son became a man so that He might redeem anyone who will reach out and accept His gift, so freely given.

O little town of Bethlehem,
How still we see thee lie!
Above thy deep and dreamless sleep
The silent stars go by . . .

Harry forgot his scars, physical and emotional. He forgot the wasted years, the impossible dreams, the unanswered questions. Instead, on this silent and holy night he experienced the most beautiful starlit Christmas service he would ever know. It was as if Jesus stood at his shoulder giving him more than comfort, giving him deep, abiding joy.

And whenever Harry looked back on this Christmas celebration in the fields, he realized that the miracle of the changing wind was a signal from God, an earnest for the days to come. It was as if the Lord was saying, "All right, son, it is enough."

That was the last Christmas Harry spent in prison.

CHAIRMAN MAO, the Great Helmsman, had died in the autumn of 1976 after a series of strokes. This titan of change was mortal after all, and when he fell it was as if the earth shook. Each man in the prison farm knew how to pull a solemn face and did so when told that China's leader had passed. But each man knew hope where there had been none, because regardless of his crime, it might be viewed differently now.

Harry churned with unspoken questions. Would this mean change? Light at the end of his personal tunnel?

Change came, but slowly. While the prisoners remained

occupied with roll call and cultivation of their assigned plots of farm land, men and women in Peking struggled for power. One rose while another fell, the Chinese dragon writhing through more upheaval. "The Gang of Four" was denounced and put on public trial.* Economic growth gained primacy. Universities, closed during the Red Guards' reign of terror, reorganized and opened.

Without question, the change that affected Harry Lee most dramatically was the occasional appearance at the prison farm of a military jeep flying a red pennant at the end of its antenna. Men in khaki uniforms rolled up in a flurry of dust, huddled with the commandant, then asked a few brusque questions of this man or that. Prisoners buzzed with curiosity and speculation.

"They're reviewing cases!"

"What do they want to know?"

"What sort of crimes are they looking at?"

Men who came with Harry from the Ward Road Prison prodded him to take action. "Hey, Lee, why don't you write an appeal letter?"

"No," he retorted. "They sent me to prison even though I was innocent. They are going to rectify this on their own. I'm not going to have anything to do with it."

"Don't be so stubborn, man. If you wait for them to take the initiative, you'll be at the bottom of the list. Make an appeal. That way they'll review your case earlier and you can get out of here."

Harry knew his advisers felt kinship with him and that their suggestions were sincere. He also knew they believed

*The title "Gang of Four" was the term applied by Chinese Communist authorities to four people held responsible for the Cultural Revolution and accused of trying to seize power after Mao's death, for which crimes they were tried and convicted. They included Mao's widow, Chiang Ch'ing.

that if political detainees were cleared away, someone might review even black marketeers, fornicators, and thieves. But a sense of justice coupled with an idealistic streak in him wanted the initiative to come from those who had wronged him; at the moment the unjust sentence had fallen, he had vowed to make no appeals.

As he thought and prayed, however, and as his fellow prisoners pushed for expediency, Harry changed his mind and wrote a letter of appeal. At the same time, a telegram came from his family.

MOTHER GRAVELY ILL. ELDEST SON REQUIRED AT HOME IMMEDIATELY.

Family letters had already informed Harry that his mother was not well. Prison farm officials, knowing his case was being reviewed, agreed to send Harry to Shanghai to attend to his mother and pursue the appeal already in the works.

So after four years, Harry walked away from the prison farm with his small and shabby bundle of possessions. But emotional release did not go with him. He was going home to Shanghai and to his family, it was true, but he was also going to face a convoluted bureaucracy in disarray. He was only one of thousands contending with multiple offices and mounds of paper.

Could he sift through the mess and persuade the decision-makers that he had been falsely accused and should be exonerated? Could he avoid the order to return to prison farm?

Caught up with plowing through Chinese bureaucracy in pursuit of freedom, Harry paid scant attention to the news that in this year of his release, 1979, China and the United States had resumed diplomatic relations and a U.S. embassy was opening its doors in Peking.

*
**

LETTERS CAME insisting that he return to the prison farm, but Harry stalled. He was free from barbed wire and armed guards, true, but his spirit was strangely still. There was still no celebrating. Part of him remained a captive. His life was a perpetual going to and fro, from court to government office, pleading, cajoling, insisting, explaining. He climbed one set of stairs and pushed open a large door upon a huge room filled with a hundred tables, a dismaying sight. Countless clusters of people buzzed and chattered and gestured with fists full of documents. So many cases, so many claims.

At last the day came, however, when fifty-four-year-old Harry Lee stood in court with dozens of others and listened to a document read aloud. It was an ordinary-looking piece of paper that pronounced him fully exonerated, innocent of all accusations. It reinstated him as a citizen in good standing of the nation of China. Precious identity papers were reissued; without them he could not work, shop, or travel.

A numbed Harry climbed the steps to the Lee apartment, drained and thoughtful. His eleven-year nightmare had ended.

THREE PIECES of paper lay under Harry's quiet hand: his sentence, his pardon, his declaration of innocence. He looked at them often, turned them over and pondered their meaning in his life. They represented a cataclysm, dividing the dreamer from the scarred veteran.

I've nothing more to give, he lamented. *My best years are gone. Twilight has fallen on me.*

Now what was he to do?

A Chinese proverb—had he learned it from Granny?—haunted him and drew him with its peaceful suggestion. "The time comes when a man puts off his armor and leads his warhorse to the sunny hills." Enough, it says. Let others do the fighting. Choose ease, anonymity, quiet.

It would be easy to do. Men with Harry's language skills were rare in China's battered society, so offers poured in asking him to teach English at universities and language institutes.

"We give good housing," they promised. "Professors receive fine apartments. What about it?"

Better housing for Mother and Edith after all they had suffered. On the day he went to prison they became the disgraced family of a counterrevolutionary. How pleased he would be to give them this! Good pay and—lovely thought—respect would be his.

So here it was. Another decision to make.

Christian, seek not yet repose.
Cast thy dreams of ease away.

These lines from an old hymn sang their way through his thoughts again and again. Harry looked once more into the face of God.

"Lord, I got my marching orders from you many years ago, orders to go forward. You know this place to which I've come. But I have no new orders that tell me to turn back so, Lord, with your help, I'm going on. I'll try again to get out of here and go to seminary."

Maybe the dreams were dead, but his commitment burned on, steady and bright.

Chapter 13

"Harry, take dinner with me tomorrow night."

Harry smiled at Mr. Ni Kuai-ting, his elderly friend and fellow Christian. Many an hour the two of them had spent with David Chen, a third evangelical leader, dreaming of ways to reintroduce Christian teaching into their community. Mutual love for God and similar experiences of persecution and imprisonment, because of that love, bonded them in a deep and abiding relationship.

"Ah, dinner is it?"

"Yes. American visitors will be there, people who want to meet Chinese Christians."

On his way to Ni's home the next evening, Harry discussed with the Lord his most recent disappointment. His twenty-sixth application to leave China had been rejected.

"Lord, when you called me I thought I could give you forty years of service. I was young and strong then. But now perhaps I have but fifteen or maybe just ten years left in which to serve you. Oh, Lord, hear my prayer! Don't let me stand before you empty-handed. I, too, want to lay trophies at your feet. Why, God, can't I get out?"

Then, setting aside the yearning that had occupied his heart for more than two decades, Harry tapped lightly on Ni's door and stepped into the older man's small rooms.

People were sitting in every available space around the room. These guests, in their love for China, had come, not for sightseeing, but to meet fellow believers wherever possible. Harry listened to introductions of the Americans with whom he was shaking hands, bemused that such an encounter was possible in post-Mao China. A remarkable change, indeed.

Here was Charles Spicer, leader of the group, a man who had loved and prayed for China long before he could visit.

There were Dale and Polly McClain, former China residents and OMS missionaries here before 1949, and Mildred Rice, who had also come back.

Then a name leapt across the bridges of his mind, a name he thought he would never hear again.

"Kilbourne? You are Kilbourne?"

Holding Harry's hand in a warm grip stood a man of medium height with a fringe of curly white hair and kind blue eyes. His wife stood beside him.

"Are you by any chance Uncle Bud's boy?" The chatter that filled the small room didn't exist for Harry Lee as he stood in silence awaiting the answer to his question.

"I certainly am." Ed Kilbourne scanned the face before him, sensing that the quiet voice and calm ways of this man masked deep feelings. Then Harry spoke.

"I, too, am one of Uncle Bud's boys."

Ed struggled to match Harry's restrained demeanor although he longed to cry out, to weep, to crush Harry Lee in an embrace. Instead, he spoke gently of the man who had marked them both.

"Father is still living."

"He must be very old."

"Yes, almost ninety. And, Harry, ever since I left for China, I've been thinking about how much Dad loved you boys who used to meet in our home. I know that had he thought it possible, he would've urged me to try to find some of you. But twelve and a half million people live in Shanghai, and too many years have gone by—but God led you and me to this dinner party. Incredible!"

So here stood Uncle Bud Kilbourne's eldest son. Memories of those lost, sweet days came washing back over Harry. Days when the Three Musketeers sat with their Booster Club friends around the Kilbourne table and talked about Christian living.

"Harry, please write Dad immediately," Ed urged. "It would mean so much to him to hear from you."

Harry wrote, as Ed asked. He also alerted the scattered members of the Round Table: Larry in London, Rudy in Sweden, Vic in Denmark, and Edward in Hong Kong.

"Guys, the old man still lives," he told them. "Write to him and tell him what you have been doing these many years."

Just two months after Ed left China to return to the United States, Uncle Bud died. "But," Ed wrote to Harry, "your letter lay open on his desk. Not only yours, but letters from all the other boys, which means he knew before he died that each of you is a faithful, active Christian. And one—you—is called to train for ministry."

ED KILBOURNE had discovered during that September evening in Shanghai that God had called Harry Lee to preach and that he'd been thwarted from reaching that goal for almost twenty-five years. Ed telephoned Leo Thornton, president of Western Evangelical Seminary in Portland, Oregon, and asked him if he would like to have in his school the first theological student permitted to leave China.

"We sure would!" Leo boomed.

"Some problems exist in this case," Ed cautioned. "He has academic deficiencies, although his English is perfect . . ."

"We can handle that. Let's go with it."

Ed Kilbourne and Charles Spicer were at that time both affiliated with OMS International, which had played a pivotal role in Harry Lee's spiritual journey. Now they were urging Harry to apply for the twenty-seventh time for permission to leave China for theological study.

Harry reflected on the months since his release from prison. He had been convinced that the Lord would open the door for him to go. When the refusal came, he was crushed. And from the debris of his disappointment sprouted doubts and questions. Should he yield to the urgings of these men and try again? How could he dare to hope any more? Yet, a fragment of conversation between him and Ed Kilbourne repeated itself inside his head over and over again.

"Harry, has God called you to preach?"

"Yes, He did, years ago. That call has not lifted. I have tried twenty-six times for permission to leave to study in a seminary, but the government will not allow me to leave China."

"We'll try again," Ed said.

Harry remembered along with this a brief exchange he had had with a woman officer in the passport office. She had taken time to explain in a remarkably kind fashion some of the current reasoning behind the granting of passports. She knew Harry was applying to attend seminary in Hong Kong.

"Hong Kong authorities have limited quotas. We are giving priority to separated husbands and wives, which fills up fast the quotas for Hong Kong. Why don't you try to go farther abroad . . . skip Hong Kong . . . it might work!"

As letters and materials he needed arrived from Western Evangelical Seminary and from OMS International, Harry began again the process of applying for a passport. Meanwhile, his heart and mind continued their quest for ways to communicate the freedom of the Christian way. This was intensified after a conversation he had with a young woman in a packed Shanghai church.

Harry had squeezed into the balcony of one of the newly

opened churches, savoring the joy of worshiping with other Christians. He shared his mimeographed hymn sheets with a girl whose clothes and sunburned face told him she came from a rural area.

Emboldened by his kindness, the girl spoke to Harry. "Sir, would you come to my village?"

Harry leaned closer, not sure he had understood.

"They sent me to find someone to tell us more about Jesus. Will you come? Will you preach to us?"

Part of Harry wanted to walk out of that crowded church, follow the girl back to her village, and preach to her people the good news of salvation through Jesus Christ. But another part reminded him that he would be almost as foreign in that village—and attracting as much attention—as an Englishman or an American. He knew that in spite of the easing of tensions since Mao's death, for him, a former political prisoner, to accept the invitation would surely bring harsh retaliation against himself and his hearers for such counter-revolutionary action.

But the girl's request stirred again in him the call of God to which he had responded so long ago. It was as if the Master were saying, "I haven't forgotten what I asked you to do. Don't you forget either."

Harry arranged for a less controversial man to preach to the expectant villagers while he continued his pursuit of the elusive passport.

THE DAY CAME when Harry received notification that he should present himself at police headquarters on matters pertaining to his passport application. A woman officer looked up as he approached her desk.

"Did you bring the notice we sent you?" she asked. Harry handed over the document that had summoned him there.

The woman pushed back her chair and disappeared into an inner office. Harry stood waiting, shut up inside himself with his thoughts and his prayers.

He carried in his jacket pocket an affidavit from a friend in America that guaranteed he would never become an economic drain on society in his host country, if indeed it became his host country. He preferred not to use it unless it were demanded of him; he felt that if he could obtain his passport without it, perhaps others following him might have an easier time of it. But the letter was there, just in case.

The clerk reappeared and tossed another order in Harry's direction. "You must pay fifteen yuan."

Harry remained expressionless as he reached into his pocket for the money, but his heart was pounding. Might this time be different from the other twenty-six? He had expected hours of hassle, questions, and interminable waits.

The woman took the bills from Harry's hand and returned to the inner office. Before he could draw three deep breaths and steady his hopeful heart, she returned and handed him a crisp, clean, new passport.

Harry glanced inside it quickly, turned, and walked back into the daylight, which was now intolerably bright. Here it was at last! God had spoken: "It is enough, Harry. Now I want you in seminary."

Marveling at the mysteries of the Lord's timetable, Harry felt the conviction that finally the time was right rising up through his shock and surprise. He questioned whether his feet were walking on pavement; it felt more like air. His mind swirled through the stratosphere as well, planning his visit to the American consulate for a student visa, plotting the route of his departure from China, dreaming of books, lectures, seminary classrooms.

His dream took on more of the substance of reality when an astonished and curious American diplomat examined Harry's passport.

"Why, Mr. Lee, you are coming to our country to study in a seminary? Amazing! Did you have much trouble getting this? How long did it take?"

Harry longed to respond, "Oh, not long . . . just twenty-four years and some time in prison." But a Chinese interpreter sat close by, listening and watching, and Harry knew that one phone call could pull him off a train or away from the border. So he decided to forego the satisfaction of revealing the irony such innocent questions provoked. He merely smiled and looked for a moment at the visa stamped into that tardy passport. Then he thanked the man and left.

Am I the first, the only person to be allowed to leave Communist China to study in a Christian seminary in the West? he wondered. *Prison took some of the best years of my life. Did I require chastisement? Why did I have to suffer all that?*

The same old unanswered questions still arose in his mind at times even as Harry, fifty-five now, prepared to leave Shanghai at last. But his conviction that God is trustworthy and righteous remained.

Maybe God wanted me in another school first, before seminary. Maybe because I began as such a sheltered, privileged person, he had to get me ready for something more . . . to teach me faith, trust, peace, unaffected by circumstances.

And as the legacy of Chairman Mao, the man who had unleashed the Red Guards on China, was being denounced by his successors in the Communist party, Harry Lee, one of the countless victims of the dragon's claws, was buying large, castered suitcases and preparing at last to pursue the youthful dream of a man no longer young.

Chapter 14

Harry stood before the open suitcase and examined what he had already packed. Clothes, things in general, had come to mean very little to him; friendships, relationships, so much more. But he supposed he would need shirts and socks and a hairbrush in Oregon.

He reached for his battered old Bible and held it as one kind of man might hold two handfuls of gold coins, another a firstborn son. Harry thought he had lost this Bible forever when the Red Guards scooped it and four others into the bag of plunder and evidence they dragged from the Lee home in 1967.

But Harry's heavenly Father always retains control of the final outcome of events that affect His children. This Bible proved it.

In line with their efforts to rectify the false accusations and imprisonment he had suffered, authorities came to Harry soon after his release from the prison farm and said, "Would you please follow us to the warehouse to see if you can find some of the things that were taken by the Red Guards?"

Surprised to learn that such a warehouse existed, Harry followed the men into the cavernous building. "Impossible!" was his reaction to the heaps of silverware, crystal, fur coats, pianos, sealed trunks, and opened trunks that spewed their contents across the dusty floor. Books, papers, photographs, letters lay scattered in pale testimony to the rejected intellectualism that suffered most of all under the Cultural Revolution.

It's impossible to find my things in this place, Harry thought. *Besides, after a man has been to prison, he comes back different. The things I treasured so much, that I clung to, those souvenirs and memorabilia . . . they've lost their meaning.*

The only items Harry considered of material value were his five Bibles, but even those, he believed, might be replaced some day if a friend should send him another.

And so, detached from the opulence of the stacks of man's treasures cluttering the warehouse, Harry scuffed along behind his guides. But as they neared the door, a second thought slowed his steps.

*If there is anything I really would love to get back, it would be our family albums. Pictures of my parents' wedding, of my brothers and sisters when we were young . . . they are irreplaceable. But—*and he shrugged his shoulders,—*when the Red Guards take things away from you, you don't expect them back.*

Harry stepped toward the door, philosophical about his losses, when he glanced toward the last dim corner. There he saw a pile of books. In the style of a true book-lover, he stooped to read their titles—and what he thought was a pile of books turned out to be his five family photo albums trussed up with string.

Harry gathered the albums up into his arms and spoke to his Father. "God, you knew just what I wanted!"

At home Harry reverently untied the string and lifted the first album away from the others, then the second, and the third. Then, in a shock of joy that he compares to a huge dollop of Hershey's chocolate atop a bowl of ice cream, Harry found one of his Bibles jammed between the third and fourth photo albums.

How did that Bible manage to get in between those albums? How could it escape the flames? How could it survive?

Questions boiled up within him as Harry relived the days

of torture and humiliation the Red Guards had brought down on his family. All he could do was to speculate about who, under what circumstances, had become an instrument of God's immeasurable love and grace.

Did one of those Red Guards look at me and wonder why Christians were different? Or why, when they screamed at us, we didn't scream back? Or when they vandalized our homes, we didn't turn bitter? Did the peace we begged God for show through after all?

And if it did, might one of the Guards while looking at my books begin to think, "Well, he's a different sort . . . and he's got these books, five of them. Some dog-eared, well-thumbed, marked all over in red. He even wrote on the margins . . . must mean a lot to him. Wonder if these books are part of the reason he's so different. Perhaps I'll give one back to him."

Harry knew that if his scenario were accurate, the person with the red armband had risked his life to include the Bible with the albums. If one of his comrades had caught sight of such counterrevolutionary behavior, the Guard would have spat out an order and the others would have fallen on the culprit like hawks on a rabbit and beaten him to death for showing kindness to an enemy of the state.

Whatever the method God had used to preserve and return to His child that precious book, Harry knew it was a gift from above.

"'Heaven and earth shall pass away,'" he whispered as he caressed his Bible, "'but my word shall not pass away.' . . . 'It shall not return unto me void, but it shall accomplish that which I please, and it shall prosper in the thing whereto I sent it.'"

HARRY CLOSED his suitcases—the rescued Bible safely tucked inside one—and embraced his aging mother once more before heading toward the Shanghai railway station.

"Harry, take a plane! Leave immediately, before they change their minds and revoke your passport," friends had urged.

"No, I can't do that. I've been away from people for eleven years in prison. I can't get on a plane and leave like that. I want to know what people are thinking, what they are talking about, what their problems are." Thus he began the thirty-six-hour train ride from Shanghai to Canton, whence he would proceed to Hong Kong.

Harry also wanted to attend one special church in Hong Kong, the church to which his Sunday school teacher had transferred when she left the mainland. Word had reached him that Miss Ward had died a few months before he received permission to leave. He was crushed by the news.

"Lord, why couldn't you give her just a few more months? Then she could have seen her Sunday school boy walk out of China in answer to her prayers."

But he knew that she knew and perhaps was leading heavenly hosts in a few hosannas as he boarded the train. His pilgrimage to Hong Kong was to pay tribute to her memory and to thank people there to whom she had passed on her prayer burden for him.

Before the border crossing and before visiting anyone in Hong Kong, Harry had to spend a night in Canton. He wandered through the streets, dragging his suitcases on their squeaking, complaining wheels and seeking a hotel or inn in which he could sleep.

"Sorry, no more rooms."

"We're all filled."

I think I know how Joseph and Mary felt, Harry mused as he stood before the last place that might accommodate him. *I could curl up on these two cases in some doorway or alley, I suppose, but what if, after I waited all these years to get it, some thief should steal my passport?* The thought was more than he could bear.

"What's the matter?" A figure in shining white stood before Harry. An angel? If so, this one wore brass buttons like the kind bellboys wear all over the world.

"Every hotel I've been to, including yours, has no room. I don't know where to go."

"You stay here for a moment. I'll see my friends." The boy in white dashed through the hotel's glass doors and spoke to someone mopping the lobby's gleaming floors. In a flash he stood again before Harry on the sidewalk.

"We found something," he announced, grinning. "Upstairs is a room with ten beds. One is empty because a man is not coming. You can have that."

Next morning, tugging his suitcases through the lobby, Harry felt full of joy and good will because of a night's sleep and a safe passport. He looked right and left for his benefactor, wanting to give him the money nestled in his palm in gratitude for his helpfulness.

But he saw no white uniform, no brass buttons. The train whistle would blow soon; his train to Hong Kong would leave. Then it dawned on him: when God sends an angel to help, the angel doesn't stand around waiting for tips.

AS HARRY APPROACHED the border between China and Hong Kong, old fears troubled his heart.

Did I make a mistake? What if Shanghai authorities phoned or telegraphed word that I am to be stopped? "Turn that man back," they could say. "We've decided he shouldn't leave."

I waited twenty-four years and then turned down good advice that I should go quickly and safely by air . . . yet I wanted to take this long and dangerous way. Was I wrong?

Border guards turned wooden faces toward the slight, graying man with two big suitcases in tow.

"Open that!" one barked. Harry complied.

"What's this?" The guard prodded a dark shape at the bottom of the suitcase.

"Oh, that's a Bible."

Silence. In that freeze-frame moment Harry tried to imagine what the guard was thinking. *"How come you still have a Bible? Did you break Red Guard rules? Did you hide it and risk your life? And how come all these people are smuggling Bibles into China and here is one old battered copy trying to walk* out?"

Action resumed, and the guard gestured toward the second suitcase. "Open this one." Harry released the latch.

"What's that?"

"That's a book to help me study the Bible." Harry had packed his pastor's old and worn *Cruden's Concordance,* which had also miraculously come back to him.

The guard studied the calm face that looked back at him across the open suitcase. He dropped his eyes first, slammed both cases shut, and spoke one word more.

"Go."

Harry nodded and walked away with Pastor Henry G. C. Hallock's concordance and his own Bible, both preserved by God from destruction. Just beyond the border guards stood a sentry. Harry approached him with the growing belief that he was truly to be allowed to go.

"Comrade Sentry," he asked, "is that Hong Kong over there?"

Harry felt as if the sentry looked on him as the dumbest mortal he'd ever waved past his duty post. "Yes, that's Hong Kong. Go!"

Harry tossed him a grateful glance, tightened his grip on the suitcases—one of which by now had lost a caster—and walked beneath the enormous red flag of the People's Republic of China.

Further on, Harry spotted a different uniform, resembling the blue of a British bobby. Was he really on the other side? Was he out? The officer's big smile reached across the space

em, welcoming Harry to Hong Kong. Suddenly
..f, Harry turned and waved to Comrade Sentry
..u the red flag. *Good-bye, China . . . for a time, at least.*
At the end of the bridge was Hong Kong, and beyond
Hong Kong lay the rest of the world—and the fulfillment of
a dream at Western Evangelical Seminary.

IN HONG KONG Harry was scheduled to board a plane
for Seattle, but first he had a rendezvous with an important
part of his spiritual roots. He went to the Kowloon Baptist
Church, which Miss Ward attended after she fled China.

The pastor greeted Harry with great warmth and love that
Sunday morning before worship. "I've prayed for you for
nineteen years," he said. Elizabeth Ward had set all her
friends to petitioning for "her boy" who was held back so
long from theological studies.

The people and their pastor pressed Harry to speak to
them, and then they wept as he told for the first time the
story of God's grace and love perfected in his life through
two decades of denial and pain.

A year later Harry received a letter of apology from the
treasurer of the Southern Baptist Mission in Hong Kong.
The letter stated:

> I was going through the mission safe when I came upon this
> letter with the sum of $1,000 HK (U.S. $146). It was put
> there by your Sunday school teacher in 1979, and was meant
> for your use when you came through. I am sorry that when
> you were in Hong Kong I was unaware of this gift lying in
> that safe. No doubt you can use it for your studies.

Tears welled up in Harry's eyes. In 1979, when Miss Ward
set aside this money for him, he had just returned to
Shanghai from the prison farm. She knew her boy was free.

She expected God to bring him out of China. She also knew her days were limited; perhaps she wondered if she would live to see him for whom she'd prayed and waited for a quarter of a century.

In any case, he imagined her saying, *I'll set aside this gift, then if I don't live to see his release, he'll still have it. And when he comes out (my boy might be like Huckleberry Finn and need shoes and socks . . . he can't go to seminary like that), with this he can buy the things he needs, and then go to class.*

Scripture sprang to mind—as it always did in crucial moments—as Harry envisioned Miss Ward's thoughts and actions. "These all died in faith," it says in Hebrews, "not having received the promises, but having seen them afar off, and were persuaded of them, and embraced them, and confessed that they were strangers and pilgrims on the earth."

After eight fleeting days in Hong Kong, after his thirty-six-hour journey from Shanghai, after eleven years of imprisonment and suffering, after twenty-four years of seeking permission to prepare for the ministry to which God had called him, Harry Lee stepped into a huge jetliner and in less than one day disembarked on American soil.

Following the pattern Harry had witnessed at each checkpoint during his journey from Shanghai, a Seattle immigration official ruffled the pages of the Chinese passport, examined the visa, looked up incredulously at the man who had handed it to him, and stared again at the document in his hands.

"They let you out to study in an American *seminary?*"

"That's right."

"Welcome, Mr. Lee!" The official closed the little book with a bewildered shake of his head and returned it to its owner. "Happy studies."

Chapter 15

May 25, 1984. Graduation day at the Western Evangelical Seminary. Harry Lee stands in cap and gown, immobilized by the pounding ovation by which his classmates, faculty, and audience honor him. They know what it cost to reach this moment—most of them have heard his story—and their hearts speak through their clapping hands.

Flanking Harry are Dr. Leo Thornton, president of the seminary, and Dr. Everett Hunt, Jr., president of OMS International, who has just given the commencement address. Tomorrow Hunt will finalize procedures to make Harry Lee a missionary with OMS, whose China missionaries played a crucial role in introducing him to Jesus Christ.

During his seminary years Harry has been led by God into missions. To become a world Christian is Harry's goal. "To go where the ranks of witnesses are thinnest, where the going is hardest" is how he describes his commitment.

As a seminary student Harry accepted countless speaking opportunities, fulfilling his lifelong hunger to minister in the name of Christ. He could not have foreseen that it would be the story of his suffering in China that moved his hearers to tears each time he told it, that this story would inspire young people to dedicate their lives to spreading the gospel.

But in contrast to all this triumph and freedom, one more heartbreak awaited Harry in the United States. His letters from Nadia had stopped when the Cultural Revolution swept through China. Even so, he prayed daily for his sweetheart as he had done since the day she left Shanghai. In Hong Kong Harry inquired about his Slavic friends and discovered that Nadia and her family had lived in Australia for a time, then moved to Canada.

He wrote to the pastor whose name had been given to him. The pastor sent the letter to Nadia's brother, who responded to Harry with the news that they had heard he had died in prison. And Nadia, possibly persuaded to believe the rumor, had married. Her son was five years old.

In a phone call that followed soon after the letter, Nadia's sister-in-law told Harry, "She married a man who looks just like you, Harry."

"Don't tell her I am alive," Harry responded.

Stripped clean now of every physical and emotional encumbrance, Harry retained a single devotion—proclaiming Christ wherever and however he could.

THREE SMALL MEMENTOS from the dark years remain with Harry, to remind him of the dragon's claws and, more than that, of what really matters. One is a scrap of cloth he wore pinned to his clothes that proclaimed him to be a "labor-reform criminal." Instead of his name, the numerals 6451 were all that Harry Lee represented to his keepers for seven years in the old Ward Road Prison.

A second is the worn pair of bamboo chopsticks with which he scraped and plucked every morsel of food from his canteen.

Third is a scuffed black belt made of plastic. As Harry moves among affluent Westerners and enjoys their hearty, delicious food, he sometimes wears that belt—and keeps it fastened in the same eyelet where he wore it during his seven years in prison lest he forget how little is required for survival.

All remind him of the past and its purpose for the present. What was God's purpose through it all? Why did it happen this way? Of course Harry asks this question and tries to articulate his conclusions at times, to explain the whys of what some would call twenty-four lost years.

"Now that I look back, I feel that 'launch out into the deep' meant so much more than the South China Sea. At first it confused me to discover that what I considered obedience to God had landed me in prison and kept me from my goal for eleven more years.

"But I needed that experience so much. I resembled the woman in a story I read. She grew up in poverty, so security meant everything to her, security that she defined as plenty of insurance and money in the bank. Security was equally important to me. I had to be certain of something before I could take action. As the eldest son I had to take care of the family. So my philosophy was 'Before I let go of this job, I must be able to grab hold of the next one.' I could see myself tightening my belt, even rolling in the gutter if necessary, but I could never bring this on my mother and sister. Because of these fears, my spiritual growth was stunted.

"But when the escape idea came along, after looking to the Lord for guidance and His will in the matter, I threw caution to the wind and launched out. I didn't know that all of that process was really preparing me for the future. I did know it was the biggest thing that had happened to me and perhaps in God's sight it was necessary, His way of pushing me out of the nest.

"Otherwise I would have been saddled with the care of a family until they grew up, sending them to college, helping them achieve that which the premature loss of our father denied them. I wanted to give them all the breaks I missed, to get Alice out of the factory, and even help Jim leave the railroad job to which he went so early.

"Another reason may be because I was too provincial, too

parochial. I needed a wrench before I could be pushed out into the wider world, to become a world Christian. If I had had my way I would have been a little deacon in a little church, quietly working and giving my free time. But we can't always stay in a little valley, a little church, a little neighborhood, a little family, a little home. The Lord certainly pushed me out of my nest.

"Now as I look back, I know He has given me a message written in blood, sweat, and tears; more of a message than if I had had my way, quietly living my little life in my little church hidden away in a corner of Shanghai. I won't say God caused the Cultural Revolution because of Harry Lee, but I will say He used it to widen my heart and my world.

"In another sense the whole experience may have been inevitable and certainly was not unique to me. If I had not been a Christian, I don't think any of this would have come upon me. If I hadn't been in a church that took a stand against sin and wrong, the Communist government might have overlooked me.

"Of course, when they took over our company and its factories they resented my choosing church meetings over their political studies. For a long time I didn't wear a Mao jacket and kept on wearing a tie. I didn't shave off my mustache. Guys made fun of me because I didn't allow people to tell me what to wear and what not to wear, what to change and what not to change. I did not believe and would not sign declarations that charged American armed forces with engaging in bacterial warfare during the Korean conflict. All this was reported. All went into my dossier, nothing favorable, all bad.

"I guess I'm stubborn. Some might call it bullheaded. But the Lord never failed me, nor did He order me to turn around or give up. And now to be able to see His hand at work on my behalf is an amazing thing.

"When I came back to Shanghai from the prison farm, my

friend Rudy asked me to send him my resume. 'I am going to photocopy it,' he said, 'and look up our missionary friends— China Inland Mission, the Oriental Missionary Society, and others—to see if they can help you.'

"But he couldn't find these people. He couldn't find the China Inland Mission because it had become the Overseas Missionary Fellowship. He couldn't find the Oriental Missionary Society because it had become OMS International and had moved its headquarters from California to Indiana.

"He couldn't find them, but in God's appointed time they came and found me. The Lord sent the right man to the right place at the right time. Ed Kilbourne was on the board of trustees of Western Evangelical Seminary. And if he and his tour group had come a little earlier, I would still have been on the prison farm, stripped to the waist, working like a slave. If they had come a little later, they would have missed me because I might have gone to a denominational college in the southern United States.

"But they came. God's timing is everything, and I felt that since we met again after forty years, OMS and I, there must be a reason and a purpose.

"Even the physical suffering and its lingering effect on my body have their purpose. I finally learned on the prison farm how to carry two pails of pig manure balanced at either end of a long pole as Chinese peasants have done for centuries; the only thing I didn't learn was how to swing that load from one shoulder to the other. Other prisoners did and thereby could ease one shoulder while the other one worked.

"It was bad that I couldn't, because irritation set in and this work finally altered my whole frame. I discovered this one Christmas in Oregon when Dorothy Backer, an OMS missionary in Hong Kong, gave me a beautiful blue sweater. When I put it on, I thought it shoddily made because it didn't sit right on my shoulders. Then I discovered that Americans couldn't make shirts correctly either. Same problem with my vests. And when I bought shoes I always had to try the right one first to see that it did not constrict my foot.

"Reflecting on all this, I remembered that while I was in Shanghai, Ed Kilbourne had brought a relative, Dr. Walter Harrison, to see me. He thought I had broken my collarbone. I looked in the mirror finally and could see, sure enough, that the bone on my right shoulder protruded more than the left one. That Christmas in Oregon it dawned on me that it wasn't the fault of the sweater manufacturer, nor the shirts and vests; it was just that this poor body had grown lopsided since all that weight had ridden on one shoulder.

"I lost an inch in height on that prison farm, an inch I really couldn't spare. I guess all that weight had pressed me down. But my bones had borne it, thank God. They didn't snap. And one day when I arrive on high, He will straighten up this body so I can wear those white robes of glory with squared shoulders.

"But if that shouldn't take place, I'll look into the hands of One who died for me and see those nailprints. I will wear crooked bones for eternity for His sake, and I'll be proud.

"Through it all, Harry Lee was never anything but a human being. Any triumph, any overcoming, is because of the Lord's sustaining grace. I asked questions at times and couldn't understand the lack of answers. But the Lord kept alive my faith and confidence in Him. I couldn't understand, but that did not shake my spiritual foundations. I didn't stop praying through ten years of applying to leave China before I went to prison, nor through seven years in Ward Road Prison, nor for four years on the prison farm. I was going to pray until my bones rested on the hills that were my comfort and joy.

"I was sad sometimes to see that my best years were gone. More than once I observed that there would not be much left of Harry Lee when, if ever, I finally got out of that place.

Sadness, yes, but the thought that cheered me was 'in his sight a thousand years are but as a day,' and 'they also serve who only stand and wait.' If this is what God has allowed, so be it. I know He does not measure as we measure, and if one fierce year—three fierce years—of work in His kingdom is His plan, then it will be my plan, too.

"God is all He declares Himself to be. The most important issues are whether we are willing to go His way, to submit to and obey Him, to take Him at His word. I did, I do, and I am not disappointed. His love and His peace have guarded my way."

IN THE YEARS since his graduation from Western Evangelical Seminary, Harry Lee has crisscrossed North America telling his story in churches, at conferences, and on campuses.

His wondering if God might give him "a few fierce years" sounds prophetic when one considers the packed schedule of speaking and traveling that fills his days and nights at a time when most men his age are taking more days off and looking at retirement property.

While studying at the seminary, Harry asked for and received political asylum from the United States government. He and his advisers judged this to be a wise action, since he felt certain God would at long last give him the ministry opportunities he had prayed for across so many years. Given his shift of residence from China to America where he is now a permanent resident, Harry is free to take his story around the world.

And the story of the Lord's perfect mercy in the suffering of His child moves, humbles, and challenges people wherever Harry tells it. When he is asked to preach, his sermons are laced with illustrations from his prison days. They communicate his ceaseless joy over God's goodness and his hunger that Christians get concerned about those around the world who do not know the Lord Jesus.

Whenever he is given the chance to talk about his mission and dreams, Harry teems with innovative ideas for spreading the Good News around the world. One of his major goals is to challenge young Christians to give their lives into the Master's hands for full-time ministry.

In 1986 Harry participated in the second convocation of itinerant evangelists held in Amsterdam, an event that thrilled and stimulated him to greater efforts for his Master. In 1988 he began to take his message beyond North America, fulfilling his commitment to become a world Christian. He spent four months preaching, teaching, and reaching thousands of people in New Zealand, the Philippines, Japan, Korea, and Hawaii.

One of Harry's dreams remains unfulfilled. He awaits the time—and at such waiting he is expert—when the Shanghai church that cradled the spiritually infant son of the House of Lee will again ring with the sound of hymns and prayers, when people can again worship within its walls without fear. He waits with hope, knowing all the while that God is there, at work, long before his dream comes true.

Epilogue

Harry's story proves that dreams do come true. They shine for everyone to see, like pearls on a silken cord, a collection of divine responses all the more precious because of their long time coming. First came freedom from prison, those dark years lit only by one bright star which through the barred window promised Harry that God was there.

Then tripping over each other in quick succession came restoration of his Bibles and photo albums; his unbelievable encounter with Ed Kilbourne, Uncle Bud's son; the Chinese government's issuance of his passport for the unthinkable, to go to seminary. Then the U.S. visa and God's protection on his journey from Shanghai to Portland. At last came three years of study at Western Evangelical Seminary. Harry finally had the freedom and the training he needed to fulfill his call to Christian ministry.

One blow to the heart awaited Harry in Oregon, however. As soon as he left China he had begun to search for Nadia, his sweetheart. He wrote a pastor friend who would know where the Russian emigrants had gone when released from China. His reply? The group, Nadia with them, had moved from Australia to Canada. The pastor referred Harry's inquiries to Nadia's brother, who contacted Harry in Portland. And so Harry learned that Nadia was married. The news hit Harry like a sledgehammer blow.

"Married?" He repeated it over and over again. "Married? Lord, you answered my prayers in such a wonderful way. I expected you to answer this one in the same way. But, Lord, you gave her to another man!"

Numbed by disappointment, Harry reviewed the times people had tried to make matches for him and introduced him to marriageable women. He had always refused because of his promise to wait for Nadia, a promise he took seriously as a Christian and a gentleman. Now she was gone beyond his reach, in a lifetime commitment to another.

Harry thought that perhaps his goal to return to Shanghai and reopen the Endeavourers Church meant he should face those hardship possibilities alone. He knew that pastors and evangelists are not on any protected species list in China.

Whatever the reason, Harry also felt he had his answer about the love of his life; it was no. Freed from his promise to Nadia, he could anticipate who God had for him instead. But Harry never felt stirred to pursue another relationship.

Later on, Nadia's sister-in-law told Harry more details about the marriage and offered that "Nadia isn't too happy." Harry covenanted to pray that Nadia's husband would find a personal relationship with Jesus Christ and that the Lord would bring harmony and peace to their home.

Occasionally Harry's public speaking included the story of his lost love, the one part of his account that had no happy ending. But God always came out the winner both through Harry's telling of triumph over pain and the joy beaming from his face.

During his second year at WES, Harry's phone rang early one morning. It was Nadia's brother.

"Nadia's husband died in a car wreck."

After telling about the tragedy, the sister-in-law said, "Remember how we prayed for him? He accepted the Lord before he died."

Several weeks later Harry felt constrained to telephone Nadia and offer his condolences. He could hear surprise and recognition in her voice when she discovered who was on the other end of the line. They talked about her husband's death and of his discovering the personal Jesus just before the tragedy. Then they found that Nadia lived near the town where Harry was to speak within a few months.

"Mother and I would be pleased to have you visit us when you come," she said. Of course Harry agreed.

Maybe I can explain things to her, he thought. *I want her to know that the first thing I did coming out of China was to search for her. I need to apologize for failing to keep our appointment. Probably she knows I was in prison, but I want to say I'm sorry, all the same. I want her to know it wasn't because my heart had changed—I just couldn't control my circumstances.*

But Harry's trip to Canada was canceled. He had applied for asylum in the United States, feeling that an upsurge of mass arrests and executions in China barred him from returning after graduation. By now he had felt God's call to take the Good News wherever it was possible to speak of the Savior. Asylum was granted, but it required Harry to stay within American borders for a whole year.

Several years sped by as Harry traveled and spoke across the U.S., riveting audiences with his quiet telling of divine rescue from the dragon's claws. By 1987 his citizenship status progressed far enough for him to travel abroad, so OMS mission representatives scheduled him to speak in several countries of the Far East early in 1988.

Wearied through he was by planes and cars, meetings and meals during that trip, when he finally dropped into yet another strange bed, Harry Lee—who had rested on bare boards, cement, hard ground, and husks—could not sleep.

What was the trouble?

*
**

It began in October 1987, when Harry had gone to Canada at last. It grew as he faced going to Vernon, the little town in British Columbia where Nadia had moved with her son after her husband's death.

What will I find? he fretted. *Has she remarried? If so, how will I feel when I see her? If not, how will we both feel?*

Harry had been told that Vernon was known as a city of widows. He worried. If Nadia worked there supporting her mother and young son, was life difficult for her? Could he, should he try to aid her?

He almost wished he could hear that Nadia had found someone else. Then at least it would be settled for all time. He would remain a bachelor. But no such news reached him and he knew he could not consider anyone else even though he didn't know whether or not Nadia was part of God's plan for him.

Harry came to Vernon to speak in the large Slavic Christian Church, a Russian-speaking fellowship. His audience were people acquainted with the kind of suffering he had known.

When Harry stepped out of his host's car on the night of the meeting and entered the church, he knew Nadia and her son, Peter, would be there. His eyes searched the crowd in the narthex until they came to rest on her face. He stared the lovely girl he'd fallen in love with thirty years before. She looked, thought Harry, just the same. And yet she was different. Changed. Mellowed, maybe. But she was Nadia, looking back at him, motionless, her eyes locked with his as they examined each other across the chasm of years—years of wandering for her, imprisonment for him.

They moved toward each other. In Harry's recollection of the moment, they shook hands formally. Nadia remembers, "He hugged me!"

But as they stood there stunned, staring, and mute, ushers

hustled Harry off to the platform. It was time for the service to begin.

People crowded into the church filling every seat. Bemused and benumbed, Harry could not keep her eyes away from the third row, where Nadia sat with her aged Russian mother on one side, her twelve-year-old son on the other. *My goodness, what a nice looking boy,* Harry mused. *He's even got a tie on . . . how nice it would be to be dad to him.*

The service lasted two hours. The older people understood only Russian, so Harry's account of pain, denial, and God's love was translated so they could hear it too. Afterward, Harry was besieged by dozens who wanted to see if he remembered them. Names and faces from the Slavic community in Shanghai came flooding back, men and women who had once been boys and girls in his youth fellowship.

Harry was due to leave in the morning for his next assignment, and the hour was late. But sensing the crowd's excitement, his host invited everyone who wanted to visit a little longer with Harry to come to an "at-home" at his place. "Come and visit with our guest," he urged. Meanwhile, the woman who'd arranged the meeting (also an old Shanghai friend) said to Harry, "We can't visit everyone, but perhaps you'd like to see your old girlfriend."

She and Harry raced to Nadia's home only to discover that Nadia had gone to the at-home and only her son, Peter, and her mother were there. Back into the car, off to the host's home. Nadia was there—but so were fifteen other people. Harry and Nadia had no chance to talk alone. Next day he was gone.

That brief, unsatisfactory encounter seemed to open up something in Harry. He discovered in himself a freedom to stay in touch with Nadia. Letters and phone calls flowed between them as they felt more and more safe communicating with one another. Just before Harry left on his Pacific tour, Nadia called and asked if he ever took holidays. "I've had no vacation since I arrived in the U.S. in 1981." "Would you like one? I'm taking mine in August. Would you like to come up to Canada? We've so much to catch up on. We had no chance to talk when you were here . . . so many questions . . . you could stay with us."

Harry agreed and blocked out the August days on his calendar. But all during his tour, traveling across Australia's wide spaces and through New Zealand's lush green, in Japan and Korea telling his story to Asians at last, Harry couldn't sleep. Even though he was filling his days with the ministry he'd longed for for half his lifetime, he couldn't sleep— because a woman with a name like music suggested he might like to vacation in her company.

August finally came. There in British Columbia Harry and Nadia began tiptoeing through the tentativeness imposed by the confusing events and years that had separated them. She had arranged for Harry to stay with friends to avoid gossip, but unexpected guests arrived at that home and they needed his bed.

"Oh, why don't you come to us?" Nadia said. "Mother is here, so is Peter, and the house is huge. It will be all right."

Harry carried a strong sense of God's ordaining in all that was taking place, so he didn't argue, but accepted what was happening as a gift from the Lord. Each morning when he sat down, comfortable and at peace, to drink coffee with Nadia, his heart told him it should have been this way always.

They promised to be honest with each other. They had agreed over the phone that each ad cold feet. Thoughts and memories and questions stirred their minds as the they reached toward each other across thirty years of upheaval and confusion.

Harry: *Thirty years ago we were young and foolish, now we're older, wiser. So much has happened. We have changed.*
Nadia: *Harry has not changed. He's still the same person. No bitterness, no nightmares . . . it's a miracle!*
Harry: *What about my work? What about China?*
Nadia: *When he spoke at the church he said he wants to go back to China. I don't, not ever. We suffered so much there. I can't forget it!*
Harry: *If the choice were left to me, I don't suppose I'd go back. But I know one thing: my church is over there and if God says to me, "Harry, I want you there," I must go back to whatever awaits me. I must obey if he calls, but right now I don't know. Maybe I will never be able to go.*
Nadia: *We're so comfortable together. Harry seems perfect to me. I know he was made so by God and I know this will continue even as we discover more about each other. We need to be patient, but the difficult times we both have endured bring us closer. We're both richer in spirit for having gone through them, and we can understand each other.*

They talked freely about their thoughts, and as they talked they discovered that each remembered a letter the other had forgotten.

Nadia had received a letter from Harry prior to his prison ordeal that told her he was ill with tuberculosis. Along with his physical problems he was feeling discouragement and depression.

"Just forget it," he wrote. "I have no job and I can't seem to leave China. We're not being realistic. I don't want you to wait for me. I'm never going to come out. I don't think I'm even going to recover. I release you."

Harry cannot remember writing that letter.

Nadia forgot that she was to write Harry when and if she married. The bleak night they parted in the empty church in China, he had looked at her tears and struggled to hold onto courage enough for them both.

"It would be best for you if you didn't try to wait for me. I am caught in this trip and I don't think I shall get out. If you find someone else and decide to marry, write to me," he whispered. "Just let me know."

Because of both forgotten letters, Harry continued to wait and to pray through the years of separation and denial.

"But in the end," he says now, "all things worked together for good to them that love God, who are called according to his purpose." Harry had painted and framed this text from Romans for Nadia when they parted. His last words to her then were, "I believe that if we are God's choice for each other, he will join us one day. If he has other plans for our lives, though, we should submit to his will."

During their two-week holiday, Nadia and Harry found that their mutual values and interests remained intact. The same revolution that had disrupted Harry's life also left Nadia's in disarray. Suffering was a commodity they shared.

Among all the world's people, in all the places I traveled, he thought as he watched Nadia, *of all the beautiful women I've met and talked with, nothing ever matched this.* Their mutual intimacy with pain bonded them together again, dissolving barriers and warming cold feet.

Nadia's parents had fled the Bolshevik revolution in Russia. In western China they were welcomed and given land to farm, and there Nadia was born. But when the Communists took over China they collectivized farms, and expatriate Russians sensed it was time for another exodus, this time to Shanghai. Their journey across China's vast midsection was like wandering from Maine to Oregon.

In Shanghai the migrants found the Endeavourers Church, and there Nadia and Harry found each other. "It was not by accident," Harry asserts. "Something brought us together."

The church and its people were immersed in agonies at that time, and the ties that bound them were forged in the fellowship of rejection and fear. But when Harry took Nadia home after evening service, he could for those moments forget misery, poverty, and trials as they walked together under the stars.

"God gave us to each other," he remembers, "her to me to comfort and reassure me; and maybe me to her to ease things a bit. And in prison thoughts of Nadia helped me to hang on just a little longer. Hope played a major role in my survival."

Now the hand of God nudged them toward each other again.

Nadia's home in Vernon lies just thirty minutes from the mountains, so one day during their holiday, Nadia and Harry drove to Star Mountain resort. They rode the ski lift, floating on air, close to God and to each other. At the top they strolled hand in hand, breathing crisp clear air and admiring the views. Harry felt like Julie Andrews, sure that he could run up and down the slopes singing the sounds of music.

At the mountain's base they discovered a little restaurant that looked as if it had been transplanted from the Bavarian Alps. Inside they dallied over hot tea and Black Forest cake. Soft music perfected the atmosphere as they soaked up the joy of being together, talking about what it was like back then, and looking long and fearlessly into each other's eyes.

Their thirty-year-old dreams were coming true at last. Then they were two young people in Shanghai with government and authorities against them, who had feared that love and marriage, togetherness, would never happen for them. But now Nadia and Harry were free, living in a hospitable world. Nadia, a hair stylist, teased Harry by claiming her theme song came from *South Pacific*.

"I'm gonna wash that man right outa my hair . . . ," but she didn't seem able to follow through.

"Well, I have a song for you, too," Harry replied. "Long ago and far away," he sang, "I dreamed a dream one day."

> I dreamed that you were here beside me.
> Long the skies were overcast,
> But now the clouds have passed,
> You're here at last.*

On December 21, 1988, Nadia and Harry were married in her little church in Vernon, British Columbia. They returned to Star Mountain for their honeymoon.

"Stars have figured in my life for a long time," Harry says. "Nadia and I walked under the stars, so happy together, back in Shanghai. Then God sent a reassuring star to shine through the prison bars when I was ready to give up. And on Star Mountain Nadia and I learned that we found each other again for a reason, that the Lord brought us back together so we can serve him as a team."

What sounds like a happily-ever-after ending to Harry and Nadia's story is really a continuation of an account of the lengths to which God will go to reconcile his world to himself. For as Nadia and Harry trek to and fro telling this story, people young and old are catching the concept that obedience matters more than comfort or safety, that the world needs to meet the Master. So people are hearing, then they're going, and they are making a difference, even in China.

---

*Jerome Kern

Harry and Nadia with Peter on their wedding day, December 21, 1988.